NEW DIRECTIONS FOR TEACHING AND LEARNING

Marilla D. Svinicki, *University of Texas, Austin*
EDITOR-IN-CHIEF

R. Eugene Rice, *American Association for Higher Education*
CONSULTING EDITOR

Principles of Effective Teaching in the Online Classroom

Renée E. Weiss
University of Memphis

Dave S. Knowlton
Crichton College

Bruce W. Speck
University of North Carolina

EDITORS

Number 84, Winter 2000

JOSSEY-BASS
San Francisco

PRINICIPLES OF EFFECTIVE TEACHING IN THE ONLINE CLASSROOM
Renée E. Weiss, Dave S. Knowlton, Bruce W. Speck (eds.)
New Directions for Teaching and Learning, no. 84
Marilla D. Svinicki, Editor-in-Chief
R. Eugene Rice, Consulting Editor

Microfilm copies of issues and articles are available in 16mm and 35mm, as well as microfiche in 105mm, through University Microfilms Inc., 300 North Zeeb Road, Ann Arbor, Michigan 48106-1346.

ISSN 0271-0633   ISBN 0-7879-5615-5

NEW DIRECTIONS FOR TEACHING AND LEARNING is part of The Jossey-Bass Higher and Adult Education Series and is published quarterly by Jossey-Bass Inc., 350 Sansome Street, San Francisco, California 94104-1342. Periodicals postage paid at San Francisco, California, and at additional mailing offices. Postmaster: Send address changes to New Directions for Teaching and Learning, Jossey-Bass Inc., 350 Sansome Street, San Francisco, California 94104-1342.

New Directions for Teaching and Learning is indexed in College Student Personnel Abstracts, Contents Pages in Education, and Current Index to Journals in Education (ERIC).

SUBSCRIPTIONS cost $58.00 for individuals and $104.00 for institutions, agencies, and libraries. Prices subject to change.

EDITORIAL CORRESPONDENCE should be sent to the editor-in-chief, Marilla D. Svinicki, The Center for Teaching Effectiveness, University of Texas at Austin, Main Building 2200, Austin, TX 78712-1111.

Cover photograph by Richard Blair/Color & Light © 1990.

www.josseybass.com

Printed in the United States of America on acid-free recycled paper containing 100 percent recovered waste paper, of which at least 20 percent is postconsumer waste.

CONTENTS

About This Publication. Since 1980, *New Directions for Teaching and Learning* (NDTL) has brought a unique blend of theory, research, and practice to leaders in postsecondary education. NDTL sourcebooks strive not only for solid substance but also for timeliness, compactness, and accessibility.

The series has four goals: to inform readers about current and future directions in teaching and learning in postsecondary education, to illuminate the context that shapes these new directions, to illustrate these new directions through examples from real settings, and to propose ways in which these new directions can be incorporated into still other settings.

This publication reflects our view that teaching deserves respect as a high form of scholarship. We believe that significant scholarship is conducted not only by researchers who report results of empirical investigations but also by practitioners who share disciplined reflections about teaching. Contributors to NDTL approach questions of teaching and learning as seriously as they approach substantive questions in their own disciplines, and they deal not only with pedagogical issues but also with the intellectual and social context in which these issues arise. Authors deal on the one hand with theory and research and on the other with practice, and they translate from research and theory to practice and back again.

About This Volume. This volume focuses on the challenges the electronic classroom offers to both faculty and students. The authors include many pragmatic suggestions about what to consider in design of technologically supported instruction and also—and perhaps more startling—some serious caveats about how quickly this instructional innovation is spreading. Faculty considering the big first step would be well advised to think seriously about the insights included in this issue.

MARILLA D. SVINICKI, editor-in-chief, is director of the Center for Teaching Effectiveness at the University of Texas, Austin.

R. EUGENE RICE, consulting editor, is director, Forum on Faculty Roles and Rewards, AAHE.

EDITORS' NOTES

For better or worse, the online classroom is a part of higher education, and comments suggesting that brick-and-mortar universities are on the endangered species list are becoming commonplace. Although we aren't sure that we agree with the alarmists, their siren calls are loud enough to suggest that the online classroom needs to be examined closely. The question is not will you be affected by Internet technologies as an educator; instead, the question is how you as an educator will use Internet technologies to affect your students.

Purpose of This Volume

The purpose of this volume is to provide information about the theories and practices associated with online classrooms. It meets this purpose by offering a variety of articles that discuss both the pedagogy and the design of the online course, because—to some extent—the two are inseparable. Even when the design of a course is not within the scope of a professor's responsibilities, understanding design is important.

Overview of the Articles

In "A Theoretical Framework for the Online Classroom: A Defense and Delineation of a Student-Centered Pedagogy," Dave S. Knowlton describes the differences between a professor-centered classroom that is based on positivist assumptions about learning and a student-centered classroom that is rooted in constructivist principles of active learning. Arguing that a student-centered online classroom is a necessity if students are expected to learn, Knowlton offers a model that professors can use to monitor and evaluate their approach to facilitating the online classroom.

In "Designing Instruction for Learning in Electronic Classrooms," Gary R. Morrison and Peter F. Guenther define distance education, explain the nature of the World Wide Web, and offer instructional strategies that will be useful to designers and educators who are creating and managing online classrooms.

In "Components of the Online Classroom," Zane L. Berge discusses the purposes of computer-mediated communication and considers what components should be used in an online classroom. He focuses on specific electronic tools and compares them with the type of content a professor wants to provide to students.

In "Making Decisions: The Use of Electronic Technology in Online Classrooms," Michael Simonson suggests that a variety of technologies are important to create efficiency in learning. He outlines the types of experiences that will be useful to students.

In "Students as Seekers in Online Courses," Mark Canada offers a refreshing personal perspective on how students must adapt their behaviors to be effective in an online classroom. He suggests that students must not be passive recipients of knowledge; instead, they must take more responsibility for their own education.

In "Accommodating Students with Special Needs in the Online Classroom," Thomas J. Buggey discusses devices that are useful to disabled students taking online courses. He also offers guidelines for designing courses that will be accessible to special needs students.

In "Humanizing the Online Classroom," Renée E. Weiss offers practical strategies for overcoming the absence of traditional methods of communication.

In "Promoting Deep and Durable Learning in the Online Classroom," Douglas J. Hacker and Dale S. Niederhauser offer five principles of instruction that have been shown by current research to promote learning and then apply each one to the online classroom.

In "Evaluating Students' Written Performance in the Online Classroom," John F. Bauer and Rebecca S. Anderson provide rubrics for evaluating content, expression, and participation in formal and informal online writing. They also offer guidelines for using portfolios in online classrooms.

In "The Academy, Online Classes, and the Breach in Ethics," Bruce W. Speck offers three criticisms of online courses and provides advice to professors and administrators for resolving these issues.

Finally, in "Epilogue: A Cautionary Note About Online Classrooms," R. W. Carstens and Victor L. Worsfold debate the efficacy of online learning and discuss concerns about literacy and the lack of human contact.

Conclusion

It would be unfair to say that the academy knows everything it needs to know about effective teaching in the online classroom. Although the online classroom is already a part of the academy and must be dealt with, it is still in its infancy. As we raise the online classroom into adolescence and adulthood, we must educate ourselves about how to be good custodians of teaching and learning. We hope that this volume will offer insights into both potential and present dilemmas of online teaching. For those of you who are already engaged in teaching online, we hope that you will learn of additional pedagogical approaches that will ultimately benefit your students.

Renée E. Weiss
Dave S. Knowlton
Bruce W. Speck
Editors

RENÉE E. WEISS *is the interim director of the Center for Academic Excellence at The University of Memphis in Memphis, Tennessee.*

DAVE S. KNOWLTON *is the director of the Center for Distance Education and Learning Technologies at Crichton College in Memphis, Tennessee.*

BRUCE W. SPECK *is Dean for the College of Arts and Sciences at the University of North Carolina at Pembroke.*

1

This article promotes a student-centered approach to teaching online courses.

A Theoretical Framework for the Online Classroom: A Defense and Delineation of a Student-Centered Pedagogy

Dave S. Knowlton

It is a daunting task to theoretically frame the pedagogy of the online classroom. Synthesizing varied new and largely untested practices (Draves, 1999) with equally varied educational theories could fill many volumes. Also, theoretical forays examining the online classroom often have a tendency to reflect the biases of specific authors, leading to myriad arguments about more than pedagogical theory; they become riddles with questions of epistemology and ontology. Although in a theoretical discussion not all such riddles can be avoided—and, in fact, some are even welcome—the goal of this article is to offer a theoretical framework for teaching online courses without discussing detailed questions about epistemological and ontological stances. Such a framework has three parts. First, I examine the differences between a professor-centered and student-centered classroom to establish the context for this article. Second, I present arguments supporting the notion that a student-centered approach is a necessity if the goal of the online classroom is student learning. Third, I offer a practical picture of the student-centered classroom when synthesized with the online environment.

Professor-Centered and Student-Centered Classrooms

The purpose of this section is not to offer a complete discourse on pedagogical theory and classroom control. Such arguments have been furnished many times in the seminal literature about teaching and learning (for

NEW DIRECTIONS FOR TEACHING AND LEARNING, no. 84, Winter 2000 © Jossey-Bass, a Wiley company

example, Bloom, 1984; Brooks & Brooks, 1993; Bruner, 1986; Freire, 1993; Vygotsky, 1978). In addition, such a discourse would necessitate an explication of jargon-laden contrasting concepts and epistemologies—for example, positivist versus constructivist, behaviorist versus cognitivist—and a detailed excursion into specific discipline-based educational strategies, theories, and methodologies—for example, programmed instruction (Skinner, 1954), situated learning theory (Cobb & Bowers, 1999), and open learning (Fraser & Deane, 1997).

Instead, my purpose here is only to offer a contrasting view of two broadly defined paradigms—as opposed to championing specific schools of educational philosophy—as they would manifest themselves in the online classroom. I accomplish this goal by using Connelly and Clandinin's (1988) model of the classroom situation as a heuristic for contrasting student-centered (often associated with constructivism and manifesting itself in the active involvement of students) and professor-centered (usually positivist in nature and most often manifesting itself through lecture) paradigms of teaching and learning. Specifically, Connelly and Clandinin subdivide classrooms into the categories of things, people, and processes. Exhibit 1.1 summarizes the contrasting paradigms. It is my contention that an online course must align itself with student-centered approaches to be educationally effective.

Things. Obviously, the notion of "things" in a classroom can vary widely. In a science course, lab tools and specimens are "things." In a geography course, maps are "things." Although it is impractical to address every item that might be a "thing" in a course, relevant here is the notion that things are sources that provide a new perspective on course material and thus better help students master the course content.

The purpose of things in a teacher-centered course is very different from the purpose of things in the student-centered classroom. In the teacher-centered classroom, professors introduce the specific things that are worthy of being studied, and students are told how to interpret them. That is, students must learn—memorize—a meaning as dictated by the things that professors introduce (Kauchak & Eggen, 1998).

In the student-centered classroom, however, students also are responsible for finding things that they can use to create knowledge and understanding. "Things" are tools to help students engage in a kind of meaning making that is active (Jonassen, Davidson, Collins, Campbell, & Haag, 1995).

I am not arguing that in the teacher-centered classroom a "thing" does not have an inherent meaning. Indeed, a map of a city does have a meaning and definition. I am arguing that in the student-centered classroom students are allowed to broaden the learning arsenal by introducing things that transcend teacher control of course material—and thus teacher control of what constitutes valid knowledge. The student-centered advocate would argue that when students use things to take more active control of their own learning, the knowledge that they discover is, in essence, created by the student. As a result, knowledge becomes more personally relevant to the student.

Exhibit 1.1. A Contrast Between the Teacher-Centered and Student-Centered Classroom

	Teacher-Centered Classroom	Student-Centered Classroom
Pedagogical orientation	Positivism	Constructivism
"Things"	Professor introduces "things" and suggests the implications of those things.	Both professor and students introduce "things," and both offer interpretations and implications.
People	Roles of professor and student are regimented: The professor disseminates knowledge, and the student reflects that information.	Roles of professor and student are dynamic: The professor and students are a community of learners. The professor serves as coach and mentor; the students become active participants in learning.
Processes	Professor lectures while students take notes.	Professor serves as facilitator while students collaborate with each other and the professor to develop personal understanding of content.

People. The tendency in the teacher-centered classroom is for both the professor and the student to play roles that are regimented and standardized. The professor is the "giver of knowledge"—the waiter or waitress who fills the empty glass. By virtue of academic credentials and professional experience, only the professor is endowed with knowledge worthy of dissemination (Axelrod, 1991). The students are the empty glasses waiting to be filled so that they can contain the knowledge that has been poured. In the teacher-centered classroom, which has evolved from the behaviorist traditions of education, the professor is a stimulus to which students respond (Kauchak & Eggen, 1998).

In the student-centered classroom, the professor is not the sole voice of intellectual authority, the only one who has been endowed with knowledge worthy of dissemination. The student also dispenses information by assuming the role of an active participant in the day-to-day rigors of developing an understanding of course materials. This does not imply that the professor is not a valuable participant in a student-centered classroom; rather, the professor's role is recast. No longer is the professor an umpire, judge, and dictator; now the professor is a coach, counselor, and mentor. Rolfe and Alexander (1996) say that when planning for a student-centered environment, the student should be viewed as the quarterback and the educational professionals as linebackers. The pluralism that is inherent to a group of students (Speck, 1998) can make such an approach valuable (Jonassen, 1999).

Processes. In a teacher-centered classroom, the professor assumes that "structure can be modeled and mapped onto the learner" (Jonassen et al., 1995, p. 10). As a result, knowledge is "transferred" from professor to student through one-way communication. Teacher-centered advocates argue that lecture is the most efficient means of allowing students to be receivers of information. Thus, the professor usually professes while the students listen. The process of the professor lecturing while students take notes dominates the teacher-centered course.

If in a student-centered classroom, however, the professor is removed as the center of the classroom, a question arises: What sort of processes keep students in the center? A student-centered approach places stock in more than simple communication from teacher to student, because this is not adequate to constitute education. A student-centered approach requires collaboration and dialogue among students and the professor (Anderson, 1998; Kearsley & Shneiderman, 1998; Jonassen et al., 1995; Savery & Duffy, 1995). Students should be actively constructing their own knowledge—discovering meaning and creating a personal perspective—by being engaged in tasks that are indicative of real-world activities: "The constructivist sense of 'active' learning is not listening and then mirroring the correct view of reality, but rather participating in and interacting with the surrounding environment in order to create a personal view of the world" (Jonassen et al., 1995, p. 11). In the student-centered classroom, students are responsible for engaging in academic "activity," whereas professors serve as facilitators who make sure the student activity occurs in carefully designed and supported communities of learners (Axelrod, 1991). Student-centered processes have yielded valuable results in a variety of different fields (see Conway, 1997; Branch, 1998; Lord, 1997; Spicer & Bonsell, 1995).

Why Must the Online Course Be Student-Centered?

It is my argument that an online course must be student-centered if the goal is student learning. This is an argument, however, that has been rejected by faculty across the academy for several reasons. Some reject this argument under the guise that "their content is static (sacred?)" and "does not change all that much" (Cornell, 1999, p. 60). The perceived static nature of the content leads some faculty to argue that pedagogy should remain traditional because it has been productive. Cornell points out that this argument is weakened by professors who are teaching ancient philosophy (static content) in the electronic classroom.

Others reject the student-centered classroom in favor of an efficient teacher-centered classroom in which online technology lessens a professor's time commitment to teaching and requires fewer resources than would be required to design and support a meaningful student-centered environment. The assumption is that professors can simply type their lectures into a file, e-mail them to students, and then allow students to regurgitate the information on a test.

As Schieman, Taere, and McLaren (1992) point out, many arguments insisting on the virtues of a teacher-centered online classroom come from pedagogues who are new to distance education. They bring with them assumptions from traditional environments about teaching and learning that are not grounded in theory. In fact, in what follows, I use a pedagogical and social argument to demonstrate why a teacher-centered online course won't work.

From a pedagogical perspective, a teacher-centered online classroom is an oxymoron in that it removes the need for the professor. In the online classroom, "lectures"—the very essence of teacher-centeredness—come in the form of predesigned text. This text may be predesigned written tutorials or e-mailed lectures, but in both cases the teacher-centered aspects of a course manifest themselves as text. If these lectures are the means for filling students with knowledge and if these texts are the "center" of the course, what role does the professor play? The student is forming a relationship with the text, not with the individual professor. These texts do not necessarily have to be designed by professors; they could just as easily be designed by instructional designers or—worse—by textbook companies. In effect, assuming that a course can be centered on the students' relationship with the text and the students' relationship with evaluations is to negate the need for professorial leadership in any form. The professor is obsolete. To put it differently, the teacher-centered "bells and whistles" are "embedded in a fancy software package and do not consider what the learner can receive and handle as part of the learning process" (Palloff & Pratt, 1999, p. 63).

Socially, the problems of a teacher-centered classroom as a framework for the online course are heightened. In a traditional face-to-face course, students are aware of a large social dimension to learning. Even when a course is dominated by the professor, students are bombarded with visual and audible clues that there is a social dimension to the teaching and learning process—students are not "alone" in their efforts to learn. The experience is humanized through the senses. In the online classroom, many students feel a strong sense of dissonance because visual and audible clues are nonexistent. The online classroom depends on student interaction and dialogue for clues to the social dimension of learning (Palloff & Pratt, 1999). This social dimension reminds students that they are dealing with people at the other end of cyberspace. The absence of these clues is dehumanizing. Socialization and humanization can help alleviate the dissonance inherent to online learning (Draves, 1999). (For a complete discussion of humanization, see Article Seven of this volume.)

It is not just humanization that is activated by student interaction and active involvement. In fact, a student's very existence depends on active participation. If students are not bound by place and time, the only visible clues to their very existence are their contributions and active involvement in classroom procedures: "If students . . . do not post a contribution to the discussion [for instance]. . . the instructor has no way of knowing they have been there" (Palloff & Pratt, 1999, p. 6), and neither do the other students in the online class.

As I have shown, the online course cannot be an example of good pedagogy if technology is used without a student-centered approach to learning. Technology is a tool—what Connelly and Clandinin (1988) would call a "thing"—and tools are meant to be used to solve problems, not just to deliver messages. Different types of technology can be used as "tools for analyzing the world, accessing information, interpreting and organizing [students'] personal knowledge, and representing what they know to others" (Jonassen & Reeves, 1996, p. 694). Because the online classroom exists solely within the confines of technology, course activity is occurring within the confines of technological tools. Thus, course activities rely on students' acts of organization and interpretation.

This argument is strengthened by Johnson and Johnson's (1996) assertion that there is an inherent tie between technology use and certain types of group work. The very act of organizing data—such as in the creation of a database—is part of "the knowledge construction process" (Jonassen et al., 1995, p. 20). A student uses a tool to yield data; the data are shared with other students who work to synthesize and interpret the data. As a result of the use of both technology as a tool and group work as a means of creating and disseminating knowledge, students are less dependent on faculty members for knowledge (Pitt & Clark, 1997).

The nature of an online course requires a student-centered approach for yet another reason. The nonlinear nature of hyperlinks both internally to a course and across the World Wide Web results in an astronomical amount of material that can be examined. The material cannot be neatly packaged by a professor and handed to students. Students must "go get it." Self-direction and initiative are required on the part of the learner to define learning and then systematically explore the online context to meet personal goals (Draves, 1999). (For a full discussion of student behaviors necessary for success in online classrooms, see Article Five of this volume.)

The Delineation of a Theoretical Framework for Action

To this point, I have provided a description of the student-centered classroom and presented arguments for why this approach is not merely a preference for making the online classroom a viable educational alternative. Instead the online classroom necessitates a student-centered approach. In this section, I delineate the theoretical framework for the online classroom. Because most of the articles in this volume focus on the practice of teaching in the online classroom, my goal is not to offer practical strategies for effective teaching. Rather, I simply attempt to connect the online classroom context with the concept of student-centeredness presented in the first section of this article and with the arguments for online courses adapting a student-centered perspective presented in the second section.

Figure 1.1 represents the online classroom. When used as a heuristic for pedagogical monitoring and self-evaluation of the online classroom, this model can help faculty members ensure that students have valuable experiences. In implementing the model, the professor should remember that while technology is inherent to the model, the focus is not on technology but on pedagogy. The emphasis should be placed on managing the learning experience, not on managing the technology (Bates, 1995; Palloff & Pratt, 1999). I recognize that to some extent the medium and message cannot be separated; nevertheless, the technology should become seamless so that professors and students can focus on course content.

As the figure shows, students are the center of the classroom model. They should interact with each other in an effort to understand course content. In the online classroom, collaboration among students is essential to promote learning (Christiansen & Dirckinck-Holmfeld, 1995; Kearsley & Shneiderman, 1998; Moller, 1998). Berge (1996) agrees and discusses student interaction both with people and with course content. These two types of interaction can be seen in different degrees. Students can communicate in one-on-one situations, but they also can engage in different types of posts that can be read by a variety of audiences (Anderson, Benjamin, Busiel, & Parades-Holt, 1998; Berge, 1999). Students can, for example, create posts for a small group of classmates, but they also can write articles that can be saved on a server for all surfers of the Web to find. The type and scope of interaction should depend on the shared goals of students (Christiansen & Dirckinck-Holmfeld, 1995).

Though Figure 1.1 shows the professor on the periphery of the classroom, the online classroom does not diminish the faculty role (Olcott & Wright, 1995). Rather, the faculty role is reconceptualized to allow maximum independence among students. The professor's role in the online classroom is *to frame* the course and supplement student interactions by providing resources and opportunities.

To frame is to facilitate students' desire to develop and implement shared goals. *To frame* is to eliminate the innate tension between the pluralism inherent in a group of students and the need for shared goals that will allow students to reach learning objectives.

One way professors can frame an online course is to establish clear goals, objectives, and learning outcomes (Palloff & Pratt, 1999). Even when the design of a course is beyond the purview of the course professor, other ways of framing are possible. For example, the student-centered paradigm can be highly disconcerting to many students because traditional courses don't necessarily prepare them for the level of interdependence necessary in an online course (Palloff & Pratt, 1999). As a result, the professor might frame student collaboration by focusing on the rationally selfish motives of

Figure 1.1. The Online Classroom

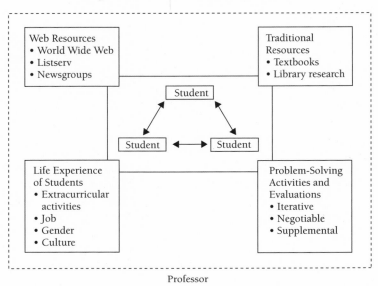

Professor

each student. Only by working together can individual students reach their own highest potential.

Evaluation of student work is another area where faculty can frame a course to help students achieve efficiency. Students could perceive evaluation in the online course as a subjective and whimsical process. This can be disconcerting. Professors can foster dialogue and negotiation about assignment criteria to help students better understand the demands of an assignment. (See Article Nine of this volume for a full discussion of student evaluation in online courses.) Framing students' interactions can also be accomplished in pedagogies that are equally effective in traditional classrooms: Socratic questioning, summarizing, clarifying, and helping students connect their ideas with course theory can all be valuable tools for framing.

Beyond the responsibility of framing, professors should supplement student interactions with traditional resources, Web resources, and problem-solving opportunities. Professors should also encourage students to contribute resources of their own and share from their own personal-practical knowledge (Connelly & Clandinin, 1988) that has developed as a result of their unique experiences. Each of these supplements can foster distinctive types of learning in online courses. For example, requiring students who are taking an online geology class to join a seismology listserv or regularly read an oceanography newsgroup can provide students with a real-world opportunity to examine and participate in a professional discourse community. Similarly, students enrolled in an online management course can offer anecdotes and examples from their respective workplaces that provide salient examples of course concepts.

Conclusion

The online classroom is dynamic; it develops a life of its own based on the course content, student personalities, and the professor's ability to monitor and guide the course and make adjustments based on students' needs, interests, and goals. Although students determine the direction of a course through their active engagement with course materials, professors must react to the direction that students provide. My hope is that professors will find Figure 1.1 helpful in reacting to students' initiatives.

References

Anderson, D., Benjamin, B., Busiel, C. & Paredes-Holt, B. (1998). *Teaching online: Internet research, conversation, and composition* (2nd ed.). White Plains, NY: Longman.

Anderson, R. S. (1998). Why talk about different ways to grade? The shift from traditional assessment to alternative assessment. In R. S. Anderson & B. W. Speck (Eds.), *Changing the way we grade student performance: Classroom assessment and the new learning paradigm* (pp. 5–16). San Francisco: Jossey-Bass.

Axelrod, J. (1991). Didactic and evocative teaching modes. In J. L. Bess (Ed.), *Foundations of American higher education* (pp. 473–479). New York: Simon & Schuster.

Bates, A. W. (1995). *Technology, open learning, and distance education.* New York: Routledge.

Berge, Z. L. (1996). *The role of the online instructor/facilitator.* [http://star.ucc.nau.edu/%7Emaur;/moderate/teach_online.html].

Berge, Z. L. (1999). Interaction in post secondary web-based learning. *Educational Technology, 39*(1), 5–11.

Bloom, B. S. (1984). The search for methods of group instruction as effective as one-to-one tutoring. *Educational Leadership, 41,* 4–17.

Branch, K. (1998). From the margins at the center: Literacy, authority, and the great divide. *College Composition and Communication, 50*(2), 206–231.

Brooks, J. G., & Brooks, M. G. (1993). *In search of understanding: The case for constructivist classrooms.* Alexandria, VA: ASCD.

Bruner, J. (1986). *Actual minds, possible worlds.* Cambridge, MA: Harvard University Press.

Christiansen, E., & Dirckinck-Holmfeld, L. (1995). *Making distance learning cooperative.* [http://www-csc195.indiana.edu/csc195/chritia.html].

Cobb, P., & Bowers, J. (1999). Cognitive and situated learning perspectives in theory and practice. *Educational Researcher, 28*(2), 4–15.

Connelly, F. M., & Clandinin, D. J. (1988). *Teachers as curriculum planners.* New York: Teachers College Press.

Conway, C. (1997). Authentic assessment in undergraduate brass methods class. *Journal of Music Teacher Education, 7*(1), 6–15.

Cornell, R. (1999). The onrush of technology in education: The professor's new dilemma. *Educational Technology, 39*(3), 60–64.

Draves, W. A. (1999). Why learning online is totally different. *Lifelong Learning Today, 3,* 4–8.

Fraser, S., & Deane, E. (1997). Why open learning? *Australian Universities Review, 40*(1), 25–31.

Freire, P. (1993). *Pedagogy of the oppressed.* New York: Continuum.

Johnson, D. W., & Johnson, R. T. (1996). Cooperation and the use of technology. In D. H. Jonassen (Ed.), *Handbook of research for educational communications and technology* (pp. 1017–1044). New York: Simon & Schuster.

Jonassen, D. H. (1999). Designing constructivist learning environments. In C. M. Reigelath (Ed.), *Instructional design theories and models: A new paradigm of instructional theory* (2nd ed., pp. 215–239). Hillsdale, NJ: Erlbaum.

Jonassen, D. H., Davidson, M., Collins, M., Campbell, J., & Haag, B. (1995). Constructivism and computer-mediated communication in distance education. *American Journal of Distance Education, 9*(2), 7–26.

Jonassen, D. H., & Reeves, T. C. (1996). Learning *with* technology: Using computers as cognitive tools (pp. 693–719). In D. H. Jonassen (Ed.), *Handbook of research for educational communications and technology.* New York: Simon & Schuster.

Kauchak, D. P., & Eggen, P. D. (1998). *Learning and teaching: Research-based methods* (3rd ed.). Needham Heights, MA: Allyn & Bacon.

Kearsley, G., & Shneiderman, B. (1998). Engagement theory: A framework for technology-based teaching and learning. *Educational Technology, 38*(5), 20–23.

Lord, T. R. (1997). A comparison between traditional and constructivist teaching in college biology. *Innovative Higher Education, 21*(3), 197–216.

Moller, L. (1998). Designing communities of learners for asynchronous distance education. *Educational Technology, Research, and Development, 46*(4), 115–122.

Olcott, D., & Wright, S. J. (1995). An institutional support framework for increasing faculty participation in postsecondary distance education. *American Journal of Distance Education, 9*(3), 5–17.

Palloff, R. M., & Pratt, K. (1999). *Building learning communities in cyberspace: Effective strategies for the online classroom.* San Francisco: Jossey-Bass.

Pitt, T. J., & Clark, A. (1997). *Creating powerful online courses using multiple instructional strategies.* [http://leahi.kcc.hawaii.edu/org/tcc_conf97/pres/pitt.html.

Rolfe, J., & Alexander, J. (1996). Student-centered college planning: The game plan. *Journal of College Admissions, 152–153,* 42–47.

Savery, J. R., & Duffy, T. M. (1995). Problem-based learning: An instructional model and its constructivist framework. *Educational Technology, 45*(1), 31–38.

Schieman, E. S., Taere, S., & McLaren, J. (1992). Towards a course development model for graduate level distance education. *Journal of Distance Education, 7*(2), 51–65.

Skinner, B. F. (1954). The science of learning and the art of teaching. *Harvard Educational Review, 24*(2), 86–97.

Speck, B. W. (1998). The teacher's role in the pluralistic classroom. *Perspectives: Journal of the Association for General and Liberal Studies, 28*(1), 19–44.

Spicer, J. I., & Bonsell, M. (1995). An evaluation of the use of student-centered investigations in teaching comparative animal physiology to undergraduates. *Research in Science and Technical Education, 13*(1), 25–35.

Vygotsky, L. S. (1978). *Mind in society: The development of higher psychological processes.* Cambridge, MA: Harvard University Press.

DAVE S. KNOWLTON *is the director of the Center for Distance Education and Learning Technologies at Crichton College in Memphis, Tennessee.*

2

After defining distance education, the authors discuss design of Web pages used for distance education and present instructional strategies.

Designing Instruction for Learning in Electronic Classrooms

Gary R. Morrison, Peter F. Guenther

There is considerable confusion in the literature, the academic community, and the instructional technology community about the definitions of distance education, distance learning, and online education. We will start this article with an analysis of the definitions and their implications for designing instruction for electronic classrooms. The second section of the article will consider the capabilities of Web pages in supporting instruction. The final section will address instructional strategies.

Distance Education Definitions

The terms *distance education* and *distance learning* are often used interchangeably. The definitions for distance learning vary from a term used to describe a more student-centered approach to distance education to a synonym for distance education (Keegan, 1996). We will adopt Keegan's definition of distance learning—that distance learning is the learning half of the distance education process.

A more difficult task is to define distance education. There are a number of definitions and each has different implications for the design and implementation of distance education. For example, Keegan (1996) notes that some view distance education as instruction that takes place in different locations; that is, the professor and students are separated by distance and time, and communicate via media. An important distinction made by Moore (1977) is that instruction (that is, teaching) occurs at a different time than the learning. In distance education courses, the instruction is prepared and packaged days, weeks, months, or maybe a year before the act of learning by the student. This time difference creates an environment quite distinct from the typical face-to-face instruction of the college classroom where the teaching and learning take place in the same time frame and with the professor and student in the same room.

Recent definitions of distance education have placed a greater emphasis on two-way communication through the use of technology. Garrison and Shale (1987), for example, state that distance education is noncontiguous two-way communication. Professors and students use technology to mediate the two-way communication. Moore (1989) explicitly states that distance learning takes place in a time *or* place different from the professor's. Similarly, Simonson, Schlosser, and Hanson (1999) define distance education as involving synchronous and asynchronous communication to connect the learners and teacher. Simonson, Smaldino, Albright, and Zvacek (2000) define distance education as formal education where the teacher and students are separated by geographic distance and telecommunication systems are used to connect the students.

These two sets of definitions are in marked contrast to one another. The first set of definitions is based on the *separation* of students in *both* time and location. The second set of definitions emphasizes a separation in *location* rather than in *time*. An increase in the availability and use of technology such as two-way interactive video and synchronous computer telecommunications—desktop video and chat rooms, for example—make it possible to have simultaneous instruction delivered to students in diverse geographic settings. If we deliver the same instruction synchronously to students in different locations, is the instruction classified as distance education? Keegan (1996) labels this method of synchronous delivery mediated by technology *a virtual system*. Distance education, according to Keegan, requires a separation of the professor and students in time and location except for occasional meetings. Similarly, the development of the instructional materials and the learning occur in different time frames. Mayadas (1997) labels some of the virtual systems as *distributed learning* or *asynchronous learning networks* (ALN). He also makes a distinction between the use of ALNs *on campus, near campus,* and *very far from campus*. On-campus use is a professor who implements a discussion board to continue discussion outside the classroom. An example of near-campus use is an urban university that makes extensive use of online discussions, Web pages, and chat rooms for students who cannot attend a class meeting on campus each week because of work or family obligations. The students might come to campus for labs, demonstrations, or occasional tests. A very-far-from-campus application might make extensive use of technology for both synchronous and asynchronous communication. Students might come to class only once a semester, if at all. Nova Southeastern University is an example of a very-far-from-campus application.

In this article, we focus primarily on the design of instruction for asynchronous strategies and self-paced learning. We will consider various strategies faculty can use to supplement an on-campus course as well as strategies for near and very-far-from-campus courses. The more independence the learners have from campus, the more the instruction will resemble the distance education course described by Keegan (1996). In the next section we consider the literature on Web page capabilities for promoting learning.

Using Web Pages in a Distance Education Course

As the Internet grows, educators have made increasing use of the Web in both face-to-face classrooms and distance education courses. The Web is often touted as making education more accessible, promoting improved learning, and reducing the cost of education (Owston, 1997). Others suggest that the capabilities of the Web can enhance the delivery of instruction (Starr, 1997). Because it is important to examine the Web's ability to affect learning, we will examine two capabilities inherent to it.

The Web and Learning. The Web is like any other software or hardware, ranging from overhead projectors to videotape to computers. These forms of technology *do not influence learning* (Clark, 1983, 1994; Morrison, 1994; Ross & Morrison, 1989); rather, the specific instructional strategy we create to engage the learner and to communicate our ideas is what influences learning. Instead of placing our hopes for a successful course in the display of elaborate Web pages, we need to focus on specific instructional strategies we can create to communicate our ideas effectively.

Design Capabilities for Web Pages. Indeed, Web pages are not inherently tied to learning. They must be solidly designed to offer students the potential for a good learning experience. In this section, we examine the capabilities of a Web-based learning environment, focusing on hyperlinks and interactive communication devices. Hyperlinks allow for learner control over content; communication devices allow for interactivity among people.

Hyperlinks allow students control over content, and interaction between students and the content is important (Moore, 1989). When students are engaged by content, whether in print, video, or other media, they are interacting with the content. Students engaged by the materials are actively processing the content, which is essential for learning. Holmberg (1986) describes this interaction as an internal didactic conversation. Jonassen and Grabowski (1993) also discuss content-treatment interactions based on instructional design strategies, which carefully structure the content to engage the learner and to facilitate comprehension.

Hyperlinks provide a form of learner control as students interact with the content. A link allows a student to branch out from the main idea to other ideas or concepts during the instruction. These links are usually available at any time and allow learners to control the sequencing of the content. Learner control is a concept that has produced mixed results in computer-based instruction (Ross & Morrison, 1989). The ability to control the pacing and delivery of instruction does not affect learning *except* for students of the highest ability (Dillon & Gabbard, 1998). According to Dillon and Gabbard, "Evidence does not support the use of most hypermedia where the goal is to increase learner comprehension" (p. 334).

However, under two conditions hyperlinks appear to be advantageous (Dillon & Gabbard, 1998). First, hyperlinks to information sources can be useful to students as they prepare for online discussions and write papers. Second, hyperlinks are beneficial when students are manipulating information or comparing information. For example, if students are comparing the voting outcomes or habits of different precincts then hyperlinks can facilitate the comparisons.

Communication devices allow another kind of interaction by creating opportunities for professors and students in an online course to interact. Interaction between learners and professors and among students themselves is important in distance education programs (Moore, 1989). In terms of learner-professor interactions, discussion through e-mail, videoconferencing, and chat rooms can be beneficial. Students find these types of interactions highly desirable. In terms of learner-learner interactions, synchronous one-to-one conversations in chat rooms allow students to communicate and work in real time with text and graphics.

Designing Instructional Strategies

Though this section deals with the design of instructional strategies, as opposed to the design of Web pages themselves, we would be remiss if we did not point out that issues such as page design and format are important. Several style guides are available to help professors plan their Web sites and design their Web pages. One of the most popular style guides is the Yale guide (http://info.med.yale.edu/caim/manual/contents.html). Some have suggested that style guides are often overwhelming, confusing, and sometimes contradictory (see Boling, Bichelmeyer, Squire, & Kirkley, 1997). Still, educators may find a style guide useful in determining the design of their Web pages. In terms of format, information can be presented in HTML or as an Adobe Acrobat file. Each has an importance that is unique.

Within the scope of this article is a consideration of the design of instructional strategies. There is a distinct difference between the capabilities of the Web and the advisability of using the Web. In other words, professors or designers of an online class must make a distinction between what they *can* do and what they *should* do. What's more, their decisions must be grounded in an understanding of effective online instructional strategies. Keegan (1996) offers a basis for making such decisions by noting the separation in time between the development of the teaching materials and the delivery of instruction. As a result of this time separation, it is important for the learner to reintegrate the teaching process while learning. In a traditional classroom, the teacher and learner are linked by interpersonal communication, which is used to help the learner develop an understanding of the content. In a distance education environment, the nature of the communication is not interpersonal—at least in a traditional sense. The task, then, in a distance education course is to find ways to reintegrate the teaching process. Professors can facilitate this reintegration by *creating internal dialogues, designing generative approaches to learning,* and *requiring online discussions.*

Internal Dialogue. Holmberg (1983) describes the use of a guided didactic conversation as a strategy for designing distance education instruction. A professor creates a strategy that simulates a conversation between the learner and the professor. This "conversation" occurs as the learner works through the instructional materials—such as predesigned tutorials or typed lectures. Holmberg's didactic conversation is similar to the inner speech described by Vygotsky (1962). Bruner (1973) characterizes Vygotsky's inner speech as language for shaping and transforming experiences. Learners can use this inner speech to develop meaning, derive implications, and make conclusions.

Generative Strategies. Wittrock (1989) describes two types of learner-generated relationships. First, learners must construct relationships among the information read in the instructional materials. Second, learners must relate this new information to their existing knowledge structures in order to form new meanings and conceptual relationships. We view the purpose of the strategies—often implemented as a study guide—to help the learner generate these new relationships between the new information and the existing information. We believe these strategies initiate and support the internal dialogue described by Holmberg (1983).

Four types of generative strategies can be introduced to students. The students' capabilities must be considered when designing generative strategies (Rigney, 1978). For example, if a student does not know how to write a paraphrase, then a generative strategy requiring him or her to paraphrase is not likely to be effective. So, introducing the generative strategy sometimes also necessitates explaining how to perform requisite tasks (Johnsey, Morrison, & Ross, 1992).

The first of the four types of generative strategies is best described as a *recall strategy.* Recall strategies can help students recall a fact (for example, the primary colors). Students can practice the fact through covert or overt practice such as writing and saying the fact aloud or merely going over it "in their mind." Another recall strategy is to use a mnemonic device (Jonassen, 1988). For example, a student needing to learn the additive and subtractive colors in photography might remember "red cars by General Motors" to remember red, cyan, blue, yellow, green, and magenta.

Second, learners can use *organizational strategies* to structure or restructure their knowledge (Jonassen, 1988). Typical strategies include creating outlines, constructing categorization tables (West, Farmer, & Wolff, 1991), and analyzing key ideas. These strategies encourage the learner to identify the ideas and then interrelate them to aid understanding. For example, students who are studying introductory psychology might be encouraged to develop a table that identifies different theories (for example, behavioral, cognitive, constructivist, and so on) and then develop columns to compare and contrast each theory.

Third, learners can use *integration strategies* to transform new information into a more meaningful form. Examples include paraphrasing the new ideas and generating new examples. A common integration strategy is to have a learner paraphrase a passage she has just read. Paraphrasing requires the learner to transform the new information into her own words as opposed to summarizing, which uses phrases directly from the text.

Fourth, learners can use *elaboration strategies* by adding their own ideas. These additions make the information more meaningful (Jonassen, 1988). Learners who draw diagrams, pictures, create mental images, or create written illustrations are using an elaboration strategy. For example, a student studying the steps for passing a bill into law in the U.S. government might be encouraged to develop a flow diagram of the steps in the process.

Online Discussions. Providing a forum for students to discuss their internal dialogues and share the results of their generative strategies can be an effective way to reintegrate teaching with the learning process. Online discussions can be useful in this regard. Shotsberger (1997) suggests that students need guidelines for online interactions. The guidelines should explain how to use the technology, suggest levels of participation, and encourage students to participate. Professors can help facilitate interactions by stressing the need for frequent student participation and by posting messages that encourage students to respond. Shotsberger also suggests that professors explore different methods by creating different roles (for example, presenter and discussant), encouraging one-on-one communication, and having students work in small groups. Professors should avoid the role of lecturer in an online discussion and switch to the role of facilitator (Jonassen, Davidson, Collins, Campbell, & Haag, 1995). If a professor desires an informal, less structured dialogue, then he or she should be absent from the discussion (McAteer, Tolmie, Duffy, & Corbett, 1997). Discussions requiring professors to take an active role tend to revolve around a facilitator-initiated question-and-response format. Such a role meets the students' expectations of an authoritative leader in the discussion but may not facilitate the interaction between learners that is desired.

Another approach to using online discussions is to create multiple boards or mail lists for a class that consist of smaller numbers of students; this creates online learning communities (Egan & Gibbs, 1997). These collaborative learning groups are useful when students need to create new models or correct misconceptions or misunderstandings (O'Malley & Scanlon, 1990).

Online discussions require careful planning and facilitation to be successful. The professor must make a switch from lecturer to facilitator and determine when a formal discussion is required and when a less formal discussion is more appropriate. Online discussions also require adequate technical support and instructions for the students to reduce problems with participating.

Summary

In this article we have defined distance education, discussed the capabilities of the World Wide Web to sustain meaningful instruction, and offered instructional strategies from the perspective of a student and professor who are separated by both time and distance. If there is a criticism of our approach as articulated here, it is that we may have oversimplified the process. The complexity of distance education course design often requires a team effort, including instructional designers, programmers, and Web page designers to name a few team members. Despite this complexity, professors in the online course need to have a grasp of all of the various roles being played. Only if they do so can professors create an environment for students that reintegrates teaching with learning.

References

Boling, E., Bichelmeyer, B., Squire, K., & Kirkley, S. (1997, June). *Visual design profiles: Making sense of the web design guidelines.* Paper presented at the AMTEC conference, Saskatoon, Canada.

Bruner, J. S. (1973). *Beyond the information given.* New York: Norton.

Clark, R. E. (1983). Reconsidering the research on learning from media. *Review of Educational Research, 53,* 445–459.

Clark, R. E. (1994). Media will never influence learning. *Educational Technology Research and Development, 42,* 21–29.

Dillon, A., & Gabbard, R. (1998). Hypermedia as an educational technology: A review of the quantitative research literature on learner comprehension, control, and style. *Review of Educational Research, 68,* 322–349.

Egan, M. W., & Gibbs, G. S. (1997). "Student-centered instruction for the design of telecourses." In T. E. Cyrs (ed.), *Teaching and Learning at a Distance.* New Directions for Teaching and Learning, no. 71.

Garrison, D., & Shale, D. (1987). Mapping the boundaries of distance education: Problems in defining the field. *American Journal of Distance Education, 1,* 4–13.

Holmberg, B. (1983). Guided didactic conversion in distance education. In B. Holmberg, R. Schuemer, & A. Obermeir (Eds.), *Distance education: International perspectives.* New York: St. Martin's Press.

Holmberg, B. (1986). *Growth and structure of distance education.* London: Croom-Helm.

Johnsey, A., Morrison, G. R., & Ross, S. M. (1992). Promoting generative learning in computer-based instruction through the use of elaboration strategies training. *Contemporary Educational Psychology, 17,* 125–135.

Jonassen, D. (1988). Integrating learning strategies into courseware to facilitate deeper processing. In D. Jonassen (Ed.), *Instructional designs for microcomputer courseware* (pp. 151–181). Hillsdale, NJ: Erlbaum.

Jonassen, D., Davidson, M., Collins, M., Campbell, J., & Haag, B. B. (1995). Constructivism and computer-mediated communication in distance education. *American Journal of Distance Education, 9,* 7–26.

Jonassen, D. H., & Grabowski, B. L. (1993). *Handbook of individual differences, learning, and instruction.* Hillsdale, NJ: Erlbaum.

Keegan, D. (1996). *Foundations of distance education* (3rd ed.). New York: Routledge.

Mayadas, F. (1997). Asynchronous learning networks: A Sloan Foundation perspective. *Journal of Asynchronous Learning Networks, 1,* 1–6. [www.aln.org].

McAteer, E., Tolmie, A., Duffy, C., & Corbett, J. (1997). Computer-mediated communication as a learning resource. *Journal of Computer-Assisted Learning, 1,* 219–227.

Moore, M. G. (1977). *On a theory of independent study.* Hagen, Germany: FernUniverstitat (ZIFF).

Moore, M. G. (1989). Three types of interaction. *American Journal of Distance Education, 3,* 1–6.

Morrison, G. R. (1994). The media effects question: Unresolvable or asking the right question. *Educational Technology, Research, & Development, 42,* 41–44.

O'Malley, C. E., & Scanlon, E. (1990). Computer-supported collaborative learning: Problem-solving and distance education. *Computers in Education, 15,* 127–136.

Owston, R. D. (1997). The World Wide Web: A technology to enhance teaching and learning? *Educational Researcher, 26,* 27–33.

Rigney, J. W. (1978). Learning strategies: A theoretical perspective. In H. F. O'Neil (Ed.), *Learning strategies* (pp. 165–203). Orlando: Academic Press.

Ross, S. M., & Morrison, G. R. (1989). In search of a happy medium in instructional technology research: Issues concerning external validity, media replications, and learner control. *Educational Technology, Research, and Development, 37,* 19–33.

Shotsberger, P. G. (1997). Emerging roles for instructors and learners in the web-based instruction classroom. In B. H. Khan (Ed.), *Web-based instruction* (pp. 101–106). Englewood Cliffs, NJ: Educational Technology Publications.

Simonson, M., Scholosser, C., & Hanson, D. (1999). Theory and distance education: A new discussion. *American Journal of Distance Education, 13,* 60–75.

Simonson, M., Smaldino, S., Albright, M., & Zvacek, S. (2000). *Teaching and learning at a distance: Foundations of distance education.* Columbus, OH: Merrill.

Starr, R. M. (1997). Delivering instruction on the World Wide Web: Overview and basic design principles. *Educational Technology, 37,* 7–14.

Vygotsky, L. S. (1962). *Thought and language.* (E. Hanfmann & G. Vakar, Trans.). Cambridge, MA: MIT Press.

West, C. K., Farmer, J. A., & Wolff, P. M. (1991). *Instructional design: Implications from cognitive science.* Englewood Cliffs, NJ: Prentice-Hall.

Wittrock, M. S. (1989). Generative processes of comprehension. *Educational Psychologist, 24,* 345–376.

GARY R. MORRISON is a professor in the Instructional Technology program at Wayne State University in Detroit, Michigan.

PETER F. GUENTHER is an instructional Web site developer contracted to General Motors University in Troy, Michigan.

3

Basic classroom functions can be accomplished in an online environment when professors use a variety of technological methods. The strengths and weaknesses of these methods are discussed.

Components of the Online Classroom

Zane L. Berge

A number of basic functions occur in most, if not all, educational or training experiences. In their simplest form these could be expressed as follows: delivery and reception of information-content, interaction between and among students and teacher, and student rehearsal and practice.

In the familiar face-to-face classroom these functions can be accomplished with technology as simple and familiar as chalk or markers and a board; books, writing instruments, and paper; and conversation between and among teacher and students. The participants can see and hear one another and the educational proceedings as they occur.

In an online classroom these functions are still accomplished, but they must be technologically mediated because teacher and students are not proximal in space or time. Increasingly, technologically mediated delivery systems are bringing the classroom, the teacher, and their peers to students' desktops at their jobs or in their homes. An added benefit of educational activities that are technologically mediated is that a record of proceedings can be stored and accessed by students asynchronously (that is, at times other than when they originally occurred).

Although the classroom delivery of instruction is *not* a gold standard against which all other educational delivery systems must be judged, it is still the most familiar to teachers and students. Educators often strive, by using a combination of technologies, to replicate this familiar learning environment. As in the in-person classroom, in the online classroom a mix of media is necessary to accomplish the educational process. The content and context of the educational experience should drive the selection of the components of any delivery media mix, but unfortunately this is not always the case. Choice is limited by the availability and cost of technology and sometimes a less than optimal solution must be used. In short, some decisions are financially or politically based—not pedagogically based.

Purposes of Computer-Mediated Communication (CMC)

Essentially, the desktop computer is used in the service of teaching and learning in four basic ways: *computer-based instruction, informatics, publishing,* and *conferencing.*

Computer-based instruction (CBI) refers to the use of computers to instruct human users, often on a one-to-one basis, and to enhance students' rehearsal and practice. CBI materials are developed, prepared, and recorded prior to student use. They include information delivery, tutorials, review and practice, simulations, diagnosis, and prescriptive testing functions. These functions can be delivered using CD-ROM discs or directly over the Internet. Feedback to the student is only that which has been programmed in, and the development of artificial intelligence to assess answers to essay questions has lagged. The preparation of CBI is labor-intensive and is often characterized by long development times and high development costs. However, there are usually lower delivery costs and greater consistency in the content and material delivered.

Informatics is a general term describing content delivery and acquisition accomplished by the use of network-accessible information servers. Informatics implies that the learner is looking for or searching out recorded information stored in online repositories, which include data file archives accessed at anonymous ftp sites, interactive databases such as library open public access catalogs (OPACs), and client-server systems that, when taken together, make up the World Wide Web and store incredible amounts of data in the form of video, sound, images, or text.

Publishing is the opposite side of informatics when seen from the learner's perspective. Instead of viewing the online classroom as a massive library, students and faculty use the computer (especially in conjunction with the Web) to publish information for others to use, comment on, and critique. Publishing on the World Wide Web makes it easier for students at different locations to collaborate on and share materials with each other. It has become increasingly obvious with the proliferation of documents published on the Web that because something can be published does not mean it *should* be published. The proliferation of documents on the Internet today leaves quality control up to the reader.

Conferencing refers to the computer's ability to aid in communication. This communication may include one-on-one conversations, but it can also include communication among large groups of people.

Component Selection Considerations

Along with these basic purposes for the computer in the online classroom, the educational systems designer must make some media selection decisions in accord with pedagogical design. These include how static the material will be, how dense the content will be, what the level of interaction will be, and whether the instruction will be in real time or not.

Static Versus Dynamic Subject Matter. One of the key decisions professors or instructional designers must make involves media selection. For information that is static—or that changes slowly over a number of years—a cost-effective means of high-density data storage can be selected (for example, textbook, CD-ROM, videotape, or audiotape). In contrast, dynamic Web pages, e-mail, and chat rooms allow for dissemination of rapidly changing materials to students. Similarly, for novice learners, prompt feedback often means that the most effective communication between students and professor occurs in real time, or as close to real time as possible, to facilitate these learning moments.

Density of Content. When making delivery media decisions, a good rule of thumb relates the "density" of the content with the time-mode and choice of delivery medium (Berge & Collins, 1993). Some form of recorded (asynchronous) delivery medium that can be viewed and reviewed is appropriate and valuable to students for high-information content (dense) materials. Media usually chosen for this purpose are books and other printed materials, videotapes and audiotapes, and "all of the above" stored on CD-ROMs or accessible through Web pages. One note of caution: long documents delivered over Web pages are tedious to read on-screen and are usually printed out by students. For individual students with their own printers this may not be an issue, but it can be a significant barrier for students who must pay a per-page printing cost or who share lab facilities with others at remote sites.

Interaction. When it comes to learning, there are essentially two kinds of interaction. One occurs when a student individually interacts with content. The other is more social: a student interacts with others about the content (Berge, 1996; Schrum & Berge, 1998). Both types of interaction are necessary for efficient, effective, and affective learning. In distance education, it is particularly important to provide an environment in which both kinds of interaction can occur. With correspondence study, social interaction about the content usually only occurred between professor and student, but with online courses it is increasingly possible for students to interact with one another, even when geographically and temporally separated (Collins & Berge, 1996).

Interaction takes different forms: between a student and course materials, between student and learning activities or examinations, between student and professor, and among students. Each student must do something with the knowledge he or she is attempting to gain. Interacting with content means actively processing and combining this content with prior knowledge. I believe that a goal of distance teaching is to create an environment that both fosters trust among learners and the professor and seeks to promote a cooperative and collaborative environment that allows students to learn from course materials, the professor, and each other. The design and careful selection of communication channels in the distance education delivery system facilitates these interactions.

Synchronous Versus Asynchronous Delivery. Closely related to the issue of students interacting with the professors and with each other is the issue of the nature of the interaction. Should it be accomplished synchronously (in real time) or asynchronously (in delayed time)?

Synchronous interaction, like that in the in-person classroom, requires that all persons involved be present at the same time, regardless of their physical location. Real-time educational activities can be carried out over broadcast or interactive television, sometimes delivered to local cable systems, by satellite, or streamed to the Web. In some "high-end" online classrooms, synchronous interaction occurs using videoconferencing. Currently, text-based interactive "chat" is more likely to be used.

In contrast, asynchronous interaction—discussion that is computer-mediated—takes three primary forms: *electronic mail, group conferencing systems,* and *interactive messaging systems.*

Electronic mail (e-mail) is unquestionably the most common form of CMC used in the service of teaching and learning. This form of communication can be thought of as "one-to-one," although most e-mail programs permit a single message to be sent to multiple recipients (Santoro, 1995). The explosion in e-mail use is based on the fact that millions of computers are interconnected via the Internet and electronic mail standards have been adopted that permit the transparent transfer of electronic mail from one kind of computer system (and software) to another.

Group conferencing systems can be usefully considered in two overlapping groups. These systems were developed to help manage some of the issues of group-oriented communication, including managing large, changing group membership lists, providing efficient distribution of e-mail among group members, providing for retrieval of prior messages, and keeping a complete record of group input and transactions. Group computer-conferencing software, whether Web-based or not, is of two basic types. One is an e-mail exploder (for example, Majordomo, Listserv, listproc), which manages group subscription lists and copies any single member's contribution to all other group members' e-mail systems. The second type of group conferencing is the bulletin board system (for example, WebCT, BlackBoard, Lotus Notes, and Learning Space). This approach simulates the bulletin board traditionally found at a shopping center or on the wall of a company. On physical bulletin boards, messages are usually written on three-by-five cards and tacked to the board for all to see. If there are enough entries, the board may have separate areas for announcements, items for sale, help wanted, and so on. A computer bulletin board usually has a number of different subject areas or items or topics in which a user may post messages. Other users may read these messages and then respond to the group or to the individuals who originally posted the messages. All messages are stored and archived on a central server.

Real-time (synchronous) or delayed-time (asynchronous) educational delivery is increasingly available on the desktop computer in the form of video, audio, computer-based instruction, and computer-based conferencing. So-called umbrella delivery technologies like Web browsers (Netscape, Internet Explorer, Mosaic) strive to make delivery transparent to users. Therefore, users' perception of multiple delivery systems or tools is blurring together as each day passes. So although it may be convenient to look at the various technology mixes in terms of synchronous and asynchronous modes, their use often overlaps both modes. For example, educational activities occurring in a classroom can be televised and broadcast as they proceed, streamed to the Web with a delay time of seconds, or recorded and stored for later viewing on tape or in digital form. Even educational activities meant to be synchronous can thus be transferred to asynchronous formats.

I have a strong bias toward asynchronous communication for most distance education. One reason is that it is quite difficult for more than a small group (six to eight persons) to manage the conversation using real-time computer conferencing ("chat"). Process training is required ahead of time or discussions can dissolve into what has been called *conversational chaos* (Murphy & Collins, 1997). Perhaps the main reason why I prefer asynchronous CMC is because, traditionally, distance education was intended to facilitate learning at any time and in any place. Clearly, if the simultaneous log-on of participants is required, someone besides the learner is dictating the time of instruction.

Robin Mason (1991), however, describes a more balanced case for asynchronous and synchronous interaction online. She cites four advantages of asynchronous communication:

- It is flexible, so students can access course materials at any time.
- It allows students time to reflect.
- It lends itself to a situated learning approach whereby students can relate ideas being discussed to their own working environment.
- Asynchronous technologies are cost-effective.

Mason concludes that synchronous systems (for example, chat, desktop video systems, MOOs, MUDs, RealPlayer) offer four equally compelling advantages:

- They are more motivating and thus can better focus the energy of the group.
- Real-time interaction helps to develop a sense of "social presence" and group cohesion.
- Synchronous systems provide quick feedback on ideas, and they support consensus and decision making.
- Synchronous events encourage people to keep up-to-date on assigned work and provide structure and discipline.

Experience suggests that a combination of delivery systems is almost always best. Using real-time and asynchronous interaction in combination will usually provide the best learning environment. The balance may be chosen based on the professor's preference and the instructional designer's needs.

Conclusions

The trend in online education is toward a Web-based, desktop, virtual classroom—the result of the text-based e-mail, mailing lists, conferencing, and chat functions available as well as the video, graphics, and audio channels that deliver interactive multimedia over the Internet. Some of the more useful delivery tools around today include HTML, page links, CGI scripting, Java scripts or applets, Active X, audio and video streaming, and various plug-ins and players (Clark & Lyons, 1999; Good, 1999). (Streaming media allow users to access audio and video content on the Web without having to wait for the entire media clip to download before they begin viewing or listening.)

Tomorrow, these tools will be replaced by their offspring and others not yet even dreamed of. The management and selection of communication tools in the delivery system allows the creation of a learning environment that helps meet the needs of students for real-time and asynchronous communication. Such a learning environment is rich in interaction and promotes learning.

References

Berge, Z. L. (1996). Where interaction intersects time. *MC Journal: Journal of Academic Media Librarianship, 4*(1), 69–83. [http://wings.buffalo.edu/publications/mcjrnl/v4n1/berge.html#mk].

Berge, Z. L., & Collins, M. P. (1993). *Computer-conferencing and online education.* [http://jan.ucc.nau.edu/~mpc3/mauri/papers/bergev1n3.html].

Clark, R. C., & Lyons, C. (1999). Using web-based training wisely. *Training, 36*(7), 52–56.

Collins, M. P., & Berge, Z. L. (1996, June). *Facilitating interaction in computer-mediated online courses.* Paper presented at the Florida State University/Association for Educational Communication and Technology Distance Education Conference, Tallahassee, FL.

Good, K. (1999). *Streaming audio and video.* [http://www.atl.ualberta.ca/articles/web/stream.cfm].

Mason, R. (1991). Moderating educational computer conferencing. *DEOSNEWS, 1*(19). [http://pchfstud1.hsh.no/hfag/litteratur/jenssen/deosnews/mason.htm].

Murphy, K., & Collins, M. P. (1997). *Reducing conversational chaos.* [http://disted.tamu.edu/~kmurphy/aera97a.htm].

Santoro, G. M. (1995). What is computer-mediated communication? In Z. L. Berge & M. P. Collins (Eds.), *Computer-mediated communication and the online classroom. Vol. 1: Overview and perspectives* (pp. 11–28). Cresskill, NJ: Hampton Press.

Schrum, L., & Berge, Z. L. (1998). Creating student interaction within the educational experience—A challenge for online teachers. *Canadian Journal of Educational Communication. 26*(3), 133–144.

ZANE L. BERGE *is director of the Training Systems Graduate Program at the University of Maryland, Baltimore County.*

4

The equivalency—as opposed to equality—of online classrooms is important. This article defines equivalency and offers steps for achieving it.

Making Decisions: The Use of Electronic Technology in Online Classrooms

Michael Simonson

> Give a two-year-old a hammer, and suddenly a lot of things need hammering.

Determining appropriate technologies to use for online instruction is quite easy: use everything available. The key to success in a distance learning classroom is not which technologies are used but how they are used and what information is communicated using the technologies. Professors must not fall into the trap implied by the law of the hammer—noted at the top of this page—by advocating one approach or a small number of approaches. Instead, a smorgasbord of learning experiences for distant and local learners should be available to students (Simonson, Schlosser, & Hanson, 1999). This advice is based on equivalency theory. After defining equivalency theory, I will propose steps for achieving equivalency.

Defining Equivalency Theory

Online students and those in face-to-face classes learn in fundamentally different environments. Despite the differences, every student should have the opportunity to learn in acceptable and appropriate ways. Some professors attempt to make experiences *equal* for online and face-to-face learners. A more appropriate strategy is to provide *different but equivalent* learning experiences to each learner. In other words, it is important to employ a variety of technologies to help students achieve learning outcomes. Equivalency is the foundation for this. "The more equivalent the learning experiences of distant learners are to those of local learners, the more equivalent will be the outcomes of the learning experiences" (Simonson et al., 1999, p. 70).

Equivalency is achieved through a variety of learning experiences that are tailored to the environment and situation in which students find themselves. It is likely, for example, that different students in various locations, learning at different times and rates, may require a different mix of learning experiences. Some may need a greater amount of observing, whereas others need a larger dose of doing. Thus, the goal of instructional planning is to make the sum of experiences for each learner equivalent and to select instructional technologies that store and deliver the learning experiences effectively. Again, equivalent learning experiences are different from equal learning experiences. Just as a triangle and square that have the same area are considered equivalent even though they are different geometrically, the experiences of the local learner and the distant learner should have equivalent value even though their experiences might be very different.

Achieving Equivalency

Achieving equivalency in learning can be accomplished through selecting appropriate technologies for online instruction. That is, equivalency theory must be applied to design and pedagogical decisions. Here are four steps for selecting appropriate technologies.

Step 1: Assess Available Instructional Technologies. This article discusses online technologies; superficially, that means a computer and a network. However, embedded within computers and networks are capabilities permitting the delivery of instruction using a variety of media. Assessing available media is a two-step process: determining appropriate levels of abstraction in media, and identifying the lowest common technologies.

First, a professor must determine the level of abstraction that is most efficient for learning. Most online messages can be stored as verbal symbols (words spoken and written), visual symbols (line drawings and graphics), pictures, motion pictures, real-time video, and recorded or edited video.

This list is similar to one proposed by Edgar Dale (1946). His "cone of experience" organized experiences from realistic to abstract. The top levels of Dale's cone listed words and visuals. They were the most abstract experiences and the easiest to use for instruction. For example, talking or lecturing about the life of a Greek sponge fisherman is much easier to do and requires fewer resources than going to Greece to work on a sponge boat for a year. The bottom levels of the cone listed realistic experiences, such as actually doing something in the real world, like going to Greece.

Obviously, the resources—both economic and technological—necessary for providing totally realistic, real-world learning experiences are substantive. As Dale implied, there is tension between efficiency (abstract experiences requiring fewer resources) and effectiveness (realistic experiences that can require many resources). This tension is at the core of instructional decisions. The professor should pick learning experiences that are no more realistic than necessary in order for outcomes to be achieved. Overly abstract learning experiences require the student to compensate or to learn less effectively. Overly realistic experiences waste resources. When the professor who is designing online instruction selects the correct media, the process is most efficient.

Second, assessing available technologies often requires that the professor determine the level of lowest common technologies (LCT). This means that the sophistication of the computer and software of all learners and the professor should be determined. Often, LCT is determined by having students complete a survey in which they clearly identify the technologies available to them. Another strategy for ensuring a standard LCT is to require a minimum computer and telecommunications capability before students are allowed to enroll in a course. For example, a 300 MHz, Pentium II computer with 128 Mg of RAM, a 10 GB hard drive, a sound card, video card, video camera, speakers, microphone, and 56KB modem or ISDN connection might be required of students.

Either option has its advantages and disadvantages. Most likely, a minimum technology level will be required for online instruction to provide experiences equivalent to traditional instruction.

Step 2: Determine the Learning Outcomes. Learning outcomes are the observable, measurable behaviors that are a consequence of online instruction. When learning activities are designed it is important that some expectations for students be identified to guide the selection of appropriate technologies.

Online environments should be media-rich and strive for authenticity; thus, it is critical that many technologies be used. It is also important that students demonstrate learning outcomes by using a variety of technology-based activities. Students may be expected to take a test to demonstrate their competence, but more likely they will be expected to offer some kind of real-world project that gives an authentic assessment of what they learned. Rubrics—which simply are predetermined heuristics to guide grading—should be available to guide students as they develop course projects. (See Article Nine of this volume for a complete discussion of rubrics and evaluation.)

One strategy used by developers of online instruction is to collect student projects and use these materials as models for subsequent students. If this strategy is used, a thoughtful and comprehensive critique of these student projects should be included so mistakes are identified and not repeated. Some developers of instruction advocate that students should begin with existing materials and redesign them to eliminate weaknesses, build on strengths, and add new concepts. Specifically, text used in a lesson could be analyzed and replaced with graphics or word pictures that are combinations of text and graphics representing teaching concepts (Cyrs, 1997). Still pictures could be modified and upgraded to animations, and synchronous chats could be made more effective by including a threaded discussion strategy that involves asking questions, collecting answers, asking follow-up questions, and selecting most appropriate final responses.

Traditionalists identify learning outcomes in terms of behavioral objectives with specific conditions under which learning will occur, a precise behavior to be demonstrated that indicates learning, and an exact standard to measure competence. Recently, learner-identified objectives have become popular—students are expected at some point during the instructional event to identify what changes they feel are important indicators of learning. Whatever approach is used, it is critical that outcomes of instructional events be clearly identified at some point.

Step 3: Identify Learning Experiences and Match Them to Appropriate Available Technology. Usually, the content of a course is divided into modules or units. Traditionally, a module requires about three hours of face-to-face instruction and six hours of student study or preparation. A three-credit college course would have twelve to fifteen modules. In an online course, the classical approach of organizing content around teaching and study time is no longer relevant. Thus, content from face-to-face courses is sometimes simply converted into online modules. For new courses, this approach will obviously not work.

An alternative approach is to organize a course around themes or ideas that directly relate to student activities or learning activities. For example, a course in history about the Reconstruction, the period following the American Civil War, might have twelve modules, each with five learning activities, for a total of sixty. The learning activities would be content-centered experiences, such as reading assignments, PowerPoint presentations, and audio recordings, or learner-centered experiences, such as threaded discussions on specific topics, research assignments using Web search engines, or self-tests.

An example module from this course might deal with the economic redevelopment of the South, beginning with a reading assignment about the economic conditions in the South. The reading would be followed by participation in an online discussion with a small group of classmates. This discussion would ask students to identify five impediments to effective economic development. When the list was agreed to by the group, it would be posted to the course's bulletin board for grading by the professor. The third learning experience in this module would be a review of a PowerPoint presentation with audio prepared by the professor that discusses what actually happened economically in the South after the Civil War. Finally, each student would be expected to write a two-page critique of the period of economic development according to a rubric posted on the World Wide Web. This assignment would be submitted electronically to the course's professor for grading.

Subsequent modules in this course would be designed similarly. At several points during the course, benchmark projects would be required of students, such as an individual online chat with the professor or the submission of a major project that synthesized work completed for module assignments.

Once the course's content is organized into modules, the next design requirement is to match learning experiences to technology-delivery strategies. The reading assignments could be delivered using the textbook, posted as files to be downloaded, or even read directly from the computer monitor. PowerPoint presentations could be handled the same way, and used directly from the computer or downloaded and studied later. E-mail attachments could be used for assignment submission and chat rooms or e-mail could provide ways to hold threaded discussions. If a learning experience, such as listening to a speech by a government official, is inappropriately delivered, perhaps as text rather than recorded audio, the value of the learning experience for the student who is forced to read rather than hear will not be equivalent and the student will have to compensate to achieve the same outcome.

In this example, the instructional media are relatively simple ones. What is sophisticated is the design and organization of the activities and the content facilitated and delivered by the media.

Step 4: Prepare the Learning Experiences for Online Delivery. Basically, there are four strategies for organizing instruction for online delivery: *linear programmed instruction, branched programmed instruction, hyperprogrammed instruction,* and *student programmed instruction.* In each case, the content of the course is subdivided into modules. The modules consist of topics that relate to one another or have some sense of unity or consistency, such as the economic condition of the South after the Civil War. The modules themselves, and the learning activities within the modules, are organized according to one of the four delivery strategies listed earlier.

Linear programmed instruction, a long-standing approach to individualized instruction, requires that all content be organized into concepts that are presented in blocks or chunks. Students review content, take a self-test, and if successful move to the next chunk or block of information. This happens sequentially until the content blocks are completed. Students move in the same order through the sequence of concepts. The teacher determines the order of the concepts or chunks.

Branched programmed instruction is similar except the self-tests are more sophisticated so students can branch ahead, if they are exceptionally proficient, or move to remediation, if they are floundering. As with linear programmed instruction, the order and sequence of instruction—including branches—is determined by the professor.

Hyperprogrammed instruction, widely advocated for Web-based online instruction, also organizes content into modules and concepts, but it permits students to move through the learning activities at their own rate and pace, in a route they determine themselves. In other words, learning experiences are identified and mediated, and students use them until either a professor- or student-determined outcome is met. Often, each module has a terminal activity that must be completed before the student moves to the next course module.

Finally, the student-programmed approach uses an extremely loose structure where only the framework of the content is provided to online learners, who are expected to provide the structure, outcomes, and sequence of learning activities. For example, students who enroll in a course titled The Reconstruction Period would be required to organize and sequence the modules and activities, and during the course to identify personal outcomes and activities to be accomplished.

Summary

The law of the hammer implies that it is simple to select media and technology based on reasons other than instructional ones. This article advocates making decisions based on what is the best way to facilitate learning. Also promoted is the idea that if teachers attempt to make instruction equal for all students they will fail. Rather, the teacher of online instruction should provide a wide collection of activities that make possible equivalent learning experiences for students using an approach that recognizes the fundamental differences between learners distant and local. Equivalency is more difficult, but it promises to be more effective.

References

Cyrs, T. (1997). *Teaching at a distance with merging technologies.* Las Cruces, NM: Center for Educational Development.

Dale, E. (1946). *Audiovisual methods in teaching.* Orlando: Dryden Press.

Simonson, M., Schlosser, C., & Hanson, D. (1999). Theory and distance education: A new discussion. *American Journal of Distance Education, 13*(1), 60–75.

Michael Simonson is a program professor in the Instructional Technology and Distance Education Department, Nova Southeastern University, in North Miami Beach, Florida.

5

The professor needs to understand the adjustment
students must make to succeed in an online classroom.

Students as Seekers in Online Courses

Mark Canada

After twelve years of attending class, reading and studying, writing papers, and taking tests, even the greenest college freshman intuitively understands what it takes to succeed in a classroom. What happens, though, when that classroom is taken away? As online courses become more prevalent, many college students have had to adjust to learning without lectures, without live discussions, and—or so it may seem at times—without live professors. Responding to an informal survey I conducted, several students admitted that taking my online Introduction to Literature course meant changes: "With other classes it has always been the same old same old," one student said. "Upon entering this class, though, everything was different." Of course, students still can succeed in this different environment—as, indeed, this student did—if they make a few adjustments.

Despite this student's initial impression, an online course resembles a traditional course in many ways. In both environments, for example, a teacher guides students through a body of knowledge and skills. Students, in turn, show the teacher—and themselves—how much they have learned by producing something, perhaps a paper or a test. Finally, the teacher evaluates this product, often suggesting ways the student can improve. In other words, education—online or otherwise—is a form of exchange. The only difference between a traditional course and an online course is the form of this exchange: traditional courses are in person with paper; cybercourses are online in pixels. This single discrepancy, however, means that online students must shift their focus in a fundamental way—from viewing the teacher as a source to viewing themselves as seekers.

Some of the materials described here are available at www.uncp.edu/home/canada.

Hardware and Know-How

The most obvious adjustment that online students make illustrates this shift. In traditional courses, a few basic motor skills are often sufficient to interact with the professor. In an online course, on the other hand, even the simple act of asking a question involves skills more advanced than raising a hand. Indeed, I ask students who wish to enroll in one of my online courses to sign an agreement indicating that they will have, before the course begins, access to the World Wide Web and a browser, an e-mail account, and the ability to use these resources, as well as others. Thus, even before they can begin submitting work to me, these online students must take the initiative to acquire special equipment and skills. Although some professors may not expect students to have all of the access or skills I describe, some may expect more. Before advertising an online course, professors may want to draft their own agreement, specifying the knowledge and skills that students must have before the course begins.

Independent Learning

The online student, however, cannot live by RAM alone. Even more important is the ability to manage time and work effectively (Draves, 1999). Monitored by teachers who may call on them or quiz them, students in traditional courses resemble athletes practicing under a coach's watchful eye; in each case, the individual can rely on immediate—and, in some cases, forceful—external motivation. The online student is more like the pianist in a private practice room; a test will come eventually, in the form of either a recital or perhaps a performance, but the motivation to prepare for that performance must come from within. "I have found that I cannot procrastinate in the completion of the weekly assignments," one of my online students tells me. "As soon as you put the assignment online, I start reading everything I can get on the topic." In writing about this course, other students use words such as "organized," "disciplined," and "self-motivated." Some students, because of their personalities, may be cut out for the independent learning that takes place in an online course. One of my students remarked: "I have never been one who needs much guidance or needs to have a teacher looking over my shoulder." But others must make the adjustment toward better time management if they are to succeed online.

Of course, just a few weeks into their first semester most college freshmen taking traditional courses recognize that they have to take some responsibility and develop effective work habits if they are to keep up with reading and writing assignments. Online students, however, require such independence and initiative simply to acquire the knowledge they are supposed to gain in a course. Although they may not always see it as such, a lecture is a luxury for students in a traditional course. In most cases, students in traditional courses have to read articles, textbooks, or novels outside of class, but they often can rely heavily on the professor to review this material, highlight key points, and ask provocative questions. Without this luxury, online students must learn to be seekers of knowledge rather than mere receptacles of it. For one thing, they must approach a reading assignment as they would a lecture. In addition to taking thorough notes that condense the material to key points and illustrations, they should continually ask themselves questions and try to articulate answers. Now in the position of being their own teachers, they may even want to sketch an outline of a lecture they would give to a group of students. Finally, because they do not receive the oral guidance that inevitably accompanies a traditional course, online students may take special care to read the syllabus and all instructions on assignments more than once.

To help students adjust to working effectively as independent learners, professors should emphasize the pursuit of knowledge—perhaps even using words such as "seek" and "explore"—when they communicate with their online students. An assignment might make this point even more forcefully; in the first week, for example, the professor might require students to do some research on a relevant topic and share it with their classmates through an e-mail listserv or an online forum. Finally, to substitute for the questions they ask in traditional class discussions, professors can post a Web study guide, where students can find study questions, lists of terms, and other relevant material. I use such study guides in all of my courses, and I frequently draw on them when creating quizzes, exams, writing assignments, and other exercises.

In part, working effectively involves students' efforts to adapt the course to fit their own learning style. Because they lack lectures, online courses may be hardest on auditory and visual learners, who will have to adjust to learning without listening to a professor's voice, hearing themselves speak in a class discussion, watching a professor's gestures, or seeing material written on a chalkboard. They also may miss audio and visual aids that could augment their learning. In my traditional literature courses, for example, my students and I frequently use maps, musical recordings, videotapes of plays, and photographs of art and manuscripts as we explore literature in historical context. The World Wide Web makes a vast amount of such material available to online students as well, and professors can make it easy for their students to see and hear this material by creating links to it from their own Web sites. Again, however, online students—especially auditory and visual learners—have to train themselves to be seekers. Even if the professor does not require or even mention additional resources, online students should take the initiative to locate and use audio and visual materials to supplement their reading. In addition to running Web searches, they should take advantage of their college library, where they can find maps, and in some cases, videotapes and compact discs.

Some online professors also convey information through e-mail messages and World Wide Web sites, and students should treat these supplementary materials as essential reading. I use a number of such materials in both my traditional and my online literature courses to explicate poetry, discuss historical context, and outline research methods. Knowing that they can expect me to cover at least some of this material in lectures, group exercises, or class discussions, many of my traditional students probably manage without studying these supplementary readings—perhaps without ever looking at them at all. But my online students must learn the terms and concepts from supplementary readings or not learn them at all.

Some online courses may require students to seek information even outside the assigned or supplementary readings. In such courses, the importance of being a seeker of information is even greater. In my traditional courses, for example, I regularly use class time to define literary terms, such as *persona, lyric poem,* and *Gothic.* In my online courses, however, I sometimes direct students to find these definitions themselves. Online students, thus, should become familiar with credible electronic and print sources, especially subject encyclopedias, and develop the habit of visiting these sources whenever they need to find a definition, clarify a point, or explore a subject in greater detail. Professors can help students find such sources by identifying several in their course materials and offering an optional library session.

If an online course places a greater burden on the students to acquire knowledge, it also requires them to work harder—or at least to work differently—to synthesize this knowledge. In virtually every course, students at some time must make connections, interpret facts, and devise arguments through writing, usually by responding to essay exams or writing papers. But in an online course students may have to write much more often. For example, in my online courses I simulate class discussion by assigning weekly essays, which students post on an online forum. After reading these essays I post an overview in which I affirm strong responses, correct mistakes, and add some of my own insights on the reading. Although some students probably contribute fewer words in these essays—about 350, on average—than they would in a group or class discussion, the medium of synthesizing their ideas in writing presents them with a far greater challenge than oral discussion. Several of my online students have mentioned this challenge to me. One wrote that she had always considered herself "a persistent, dedicated, and driven individual," but revealed that the format of this course tested her in ways she "never thought would be possible." She went on to say: "The assignments were quite clear as they were posted, but they required extensive thought and research." Noting both reading and writing assignments, another student said: "It almost seems there is a trade-off. If you are given the opportunity of an online course and there is no travel time or attendance, then you will pay for this convenience with massive amounts of work. I have thoroughly enjoyed this online course, but to be honest, I feel that for a three-credit hour course, I have worked my buns off."

Thus, in the case of some online courses, students may need to adjust to thinking through and articulating their ideas primarily in writing rather than through oral discussion. Of course, this format may be a draw for some students. Two of mine have said that they enjoy writing, and one even mentioned that written discussion was a nice change of pace for him because his stuttering problem had inhibited him during traditional oral discussions in other courses. Again, professors can ease the transition. For example, I use e-mail to respond to every student's first writing assignment, noting strengths and areas for improvement. I then periodically respond to later assignments throughout the semester.

A Personal Touch

Although online courses in many ways force students to work more independently, they also require a greater effort to connect with other people. "The only adverse part of this course," one student lamented, "is that you don't know me and I don't know you. Voices only. When teaching any class, I think the passion and professor's actions communicate a lot about what he or she is attempting to teach. With an online class you miss that." Another student pointed out: "In the classroom, a professor is able to pass on to his students any personal experiences and knowledge that he has encountered in his career. Unfortunately, students in an online course do not have this extra insight that a professor can add to a class."

A human being with feelings, experiences, and maybe even a knack for performing, a professor in a traditional classroom can bring material alive simply by being alive. Furthermore, by connecting with students on a human level, a professor can help a student remain interested and actively engaged in a course, especially when personal pressures may threaten the student's success. Without a personal presence in the classroom, online students should make an extra effort to connect with their professors and classmates. Professors can facilitate connections in a number of ways. At the beginning of my online courses, I invite students to visit my personal Web pages, where they can find news about my family, home, and interests. I also ask them to introduce themselves to me and to each other by submitting a brief note to the online forum. Of course, such electronic connections cannot fully substitute for personal interaction, which professors can encourage by inviting students to visit them during their office hours. More ambitious professors may want to schedule optional or mandatory gatherings to explore library resources, view a videotape or an art exhibit, or simply eat lunch in the school cafeteria and talk. (See Article Seven for additional information on helping students make personal connections in the online classroom.)

Conclusion

The recent trend in education has been toward the student-centered classroom. Rather than listen to a professor lecture for virtually all of every class, students have become accustomed to seeking, synthesizing, and articulating knowledge in the classroom. With their emphasis on independent learning, online courses are the culmination of this trend. Professors of these courses can do a tremendous service to their students by helping them learn to take initiative and responsibility—two qualities that will serve them well in their other courses as well as in the rest of their lives.

Reference

Draves, W. A. (1999). Why learning online is totally different. *Lifelong Learning Today, 3*, 4–8.

MARK CANADA is an assistant professor of English at the University of North Carolina at Pembroke.

6

Online classrooms must offer reasonable accommodation for students with disabilities. This article discusses the legal basis for accommodation, describes useful assistive technologies, and offers advice for designing online courses that can accommodate students with a range of disabilities.

Accommodating Students with Special Needs in the Online Classroom

Thomas J. Buggey

When planning online classrooms, professors need to consider factors that will enable students with disabilities to participate fully in all aspects of the course. Approximately one in five persons in the United States has a diagnosed disability and this population constitutes about 8 percent of all Web users (Capozzi, 1998). The number of people with disabilities enrolled in higher education is growing rapidly thanks to better support services at colleges; high school and elementary programs that offer curricular adaptations to accommodate diverse learners; and accessibility to, and development of, assistive technologies. (*Assistive technology* refers to any device that enables people with disabilities to function better in their environment.) Although these factors are important, the groundwork to promote the enrollment of persons with disabilities in higher education was done by federal legislation that mandated equal access opportunities.

Federal Laws Ensuring Equal Opportunity Access

Most of the federal laws associated with disability issues can be traced to the 1954 Supreme Court ruling in *Brown v. Topeka Board of Education*. In this landmark civil rights case, the Court ruled that equality cannot be achieved when a minority is segregated from the rest of society. The precedent established led to a spate of litigation on behalf of persons with disabilities. These successful suits, in turn, resulted in federal laws protecting the rights of this population.

Two of these laws are especially relevant to professors in higher education: the Rehabilitation Act of 1973 and the Americans with Disabilities Act of 1990. Because of the Americans with Disabilities Act (ADA), universities have made changes to physical structures and established systems of academic support for their students with disabilities—including equal access to computers on public campuses (Wilson, Kotlas, & Martin, 1994). When designing online courses, the same access criteria apply. A crack in the sidewalk is analogous to many access issues on the Internet. Designers must visualize the cyberclassroom in a manner similar to the traditional three-dimensional classroom in terms of accessibility. Any barrier standing in the way of a person's participation should be removed.

In 1996 Deval L. Patrick, assistant attorney general in the civil rights division of the Department of Justice, communicated the interpretation of how the ADA relates to Internet access:

> State and local governments' entities subject to title II or places of public accommodation subject to title III of the ADA that use the Internet to provide information regarding their programs, goods, or services must be prepared to offer those communications through accessible means. Such entities may provide Web page information in text format that is accessible to screen reading devices that are used by people with visual impairments, and they may also offer alternative accessible formats that are identified in a screen-readable format on a Web page. [Capozzi, 1998, p. 1]

The Office of Civil Rights has ruled that universities and other public entities cannot apply accommodations under ADA on an ad hoc or individual case basis (Waddell, 1998). Thus, plans and designs for online courses should include considerations that will accommodate a variety of disabling conditions. In an effort to ensure universal access to all forms of electronic media, the U.S. government has taken the initiative to develop rules and guidelines to facilitate and standardize the process.

In 1986, Congress amended the Rehabilitation Act and added section 508, which required the Department of Education and the General Services Administration to develop accessibility guidelines for all electronic and information technology purchased by federal agencies (Library of Congress, 1999). Although this law did not directly affect any agencies outside the federal government, it marked the beginning of an effort to establish and standardize a format for guaranteeing equal access to persons with disabilities.

Online college classes are not addressed directly in federal laws, but clearly any such course that does not provide access for students with disabilities would be in violation of the ADA and the Rehabilitation Act. (For an extensive resource about legal and accessibility issues, visit www.empowermentzone.com/techlaws.txt.)

Assistive Technologies That Enable Online Participation

Eyeglasses, wheelchairs, and hearing aids are assistive devices that have long histories; however, the computer age has spawned rapid growth in microchip and electronic technology that has directly affected the degree to which persons with disabilities can participate in the community. It is assistive technology that allows Stephen Hawking, the Isaac Newton Chair of Mathematics at Cambridge University who has Amyotrophic Lateral Sclerosis, to continue his research into the physics of the beginning of'the universe.

Assistive computing is defined as any method or device that makes the computer more accessible for a user with a disability. Hardware adaptations include special ability switches, touch- or light-activated keyboards and screens for those with mobility impairments, screen magnification systems, and large-print screen displays for those with poor vision.

Switch technology allows persons with even severe physical disabilities to have full access to computers. Switches are designed to work with any area of the body that has some voluntary movement. Commercial switches that can respond to eyebrow movements and even the inhalation patterns of users are available. With the addition of scanning software, the whole computer, and thus the World Wide Web, becomes accessible literally at the flick of a switch. Scanning software allows the user to move the cursor repeatedly from one character, or group of characters, to the next. As the cursor falls on the correct character or word, the user presses the switch to make a selection.

People with visual impairments also have a variety of peripheral devices that enable them to access online materials. Large-print screen displays are created either through stand-alone software programs, or hardware- and software-based magnification systems (Wilson et al., 1994). Screen magnifying systems employ both hardware and software adaptations to magnify the screen display. Braille computer systems consist of hardware devices that allow access to the screen display by translating it line-by-line into a tactile Braille display. Several types of printer systems also allow persons with visual impairments to access text and images in a three-dimensional form (Anson, 1997).

The number and variety of assistive computing devices available for persons with disabilities are expanding rapidly. As this population transitions further into the mainstream, and as employers and service providers come into compliance with disability-related laws, the market for assistive devices will increase. This technology will help persons with disabilities function successfully in online courses.

Designing an Accessible Online Course

Assistive technologies alone will not always provide accessibility to disabled students, however. Online courses must be designed to provide accommodation. In May 1999, the Web Access Initiative of the World Wide Web Consortium (W3C) published the *Web Content Accessibility Guidelines* (Chisholm, Vanderheiden, & Jacobs, 1999). This publication was a culmination of collaborative efforts of groups from around the world. At present it is the definitive reference on providing universal access to the Internet and an essential document for those who wish to develop online courses. The complete text of the guidelines is available at www.w3.org/TR/WAI-WEBCONTENT/. The guidelines are too extensive for inclusion here in their entirety, but an understanding of the general ideas of the document will allow course designers to make basic adaptations.

Keep It Simple. The universal use of Hyper Text Markup Language (HTML) has made the Internet far more accessible. HTML allows access through a range of Web browsers and facilitates screen reading by peripheral devices. With the introduction of Java and other design tools, however, developers have gone from a keep-it-simple mode to the "bells, buttons, and flickering flames" mode. When designing for universal access, these "cute" additions can create significant barriers. The keep-it-simple mode should be the design choice for online course developers.

It is important, for example, that page layout across the site is consistent and that the navigation system is easily accessible. As a backup to ensure ease of navigation, an alternate page with access instructions could be included. This page should contain an e-mail link for those with questions or those who are experiencing problems (Waddell, 1998).

Design for Students with Specific Disabilities. The most common disabilities limiting college students' access to computers are impairments of hearing, vision, and mobility (Wilson et al., 1994). Specific design strategies can assist students with these disabilities.

Students with hearing impairments usually require the lowest modification because of the highly visual nature of the Internet. However, accommodations are required when movie or audio clips are included in courses. Links to text transcripts of the clips are a simple solution to this barrier.

Students with visual impairments will obviously have difficulty interpreting images and icons. The "Alt" tag in HTML, which provides a convenient supplement to graphic images, was first provided to accommodate text-only browsers but serves a dual purpose for those with visual impairments. Screen readers and Braille displays can read descriptions of any images. If the descriptions are too lengthy for easy inclusion with the "Alt" tag, the "longdesc" tag or a link with descriptive text should be included.

PDF, table, newspaper, and frame formats are not as accessible as HTML. These formats break up the left to right sequences necessary for most screen readers. If posting in one of these other formats is necessary, it is necessary to provide access to HTML text or ASCII files. Forms can also be made accessible by providing ones that can be downloaded and then mailed or e-mailed, or by providing a phone number that users can call to obtain the information (Shumila, 1999).

The keep-it-simple concept suggests that background colors should contrast well with text. People with visual impairments may have difficulty discriminating print that is embedded in distracting backgrounds. When a multimedia presentation is made, an audio track should be included that provides a description of the important information in the presentation. Additional information on designing Web pages for persons who are blind or visually impaired can be accessed at www.scils.rutgers.edu /~mowalker /access05.htm.

Persons with physical disabilities need few adaptations if they are fitted with appropriate assistive technology. However, a situation that may still require adaptation is when rapid input is involved, such as in teleconferencing or chat rooms. Scanning through the alphabet one letter at a time can take a great deal of time. But if the student is provided with prewritten discussion questions or topics, that will facilitate his or her preparation and participation.

Some course content may not be transferable to alternative access over the Internet. When all else fails, it is important to provide a text-only version of the course site and arrange personal accommodations directly with the students in question. When planning for accommodations, it is important to focus on equality. For example, if a professor is planning a teleconference that may raise participation barriers for a particular student, the professor must first consider how to involve the student in the conference. As stated earlier, this may require presentation of topics and questions so that a person using a scanning device can prepare a range of possible responses. Providing alternative activities is unacceptable, however, unless this opportunity is presented as an option for the entire class.

Measure Accessibility. There are several ways to determine if a Web site or online course is accessible. "Bobby" is a software program that evaluates sites for accessibility. It is downloadable from the Center for Applied Special Technology (CAST), at www.cast.org/bobby/. Results from "Bobby" include a line-by-line site analysis with recommendations for improvement. Developers can also do manual checks by using a text-only browser such as Lynx. Probably the best way for professors to check accessibility is to contact the disability support department on their campus. Students or the support staff can attempt to access the course with their assistive devices. Professors who do this not only get constructive feedback but also gain experience and knowledge of their ultimate consumers.

Conclusion

Online courses offer a unique opportunity for some with disabilities. The computer can be the great equalizer. Persons who are medically fragile and could not physically attend classes may finally have a chance to get their degrees. At all levels of education, the inclusion of students with disabilities has led to changes in the attitudes of their classmates. Persons without disabilities develop empathy and tolerance for those who are different—which is probably one of the foremost goals listed on the mission statement of most universities.

References

Anson, D. K. (1997). *Alternative computer access: A guide to selection.* Worcester, MA: Davis.

Capozzi, D. (February 19, 1998). *Technology access by citizens with disabilities.* Speech presented at the Microsoft Accessibility Summit. Redmond, WA.

Chisholm, W., Vanderheiden, G., & Jacobs, I. (1999). *Web content accessibility guidelines.* World Wide Web Consortium. [[http://www.w3.org/TR/1999/WAI-WEBCONTENT].

Library of Congress. (1999). *THOMAS: Legislative information on the Internet.* [http://thomas.loc.gov/cgi-bin/query/D?c104:3:./temp/~c104mwbVlv::].

Shumila, D. (1999). *HTML commandments.* [http://www.utoronto.ca/atrc/rd/html/commandments.html].

Waddell, C. D. (June 17, 1998). *Applying the ADA to the Internet: A Web accessibility standard.* Paper presented at the American Bar Association's National Conference "In Pursuit of a Blueprint for Disability Law and Policy," Toronto.

Wilson, L., Kotlas, C., & Martin, M. (1994). *Assistive technology for the disabled computer user.* Falls Church, VA: Conwal Incorporated.

THOMAS J. BUGGEY *is an associate professor in the Department of Instruction and Curriculum Leadership at The University of Memphis in Memphis, Tennessee.*

7

Without proper planning, the cyberclassroom can seem remote and impersonal. This article offers advice for humanizing the classroom, making it a more personal experience for students and professors alike.

Humanizing the Online Classroom

Renée E. Weiss

A concern among educators who have considered online learning is the loss of personal contact between them and the students and among the students themselves. (See Article Eleven for an in-depth discussion of this and related issues.) The thoughtful professor knows that teaching is not simply a matter of delivering a commodity as one would deliver a pound of meat or broccoli; teaching is infinitely more complex because in many subjects it also involves leading the student to analyze, synthesize, and exercise critical judgments (Neal, 1998; Palloff & Pratt, 1999). These advanced skills require a high amount of interaction between professor and student, as well as collaboration among students. How can professors of online courses ensure quality interaction despite the loss of personal contact? To answer this question, this article will analyze the problems introduced by distance learning and then offer possible solutions to these problems.

The Problems

An obvious deficiency of any course that uses only text and graphics is the loss of auditory inflections that we take for granted in our daily personal contacts. Sometimes it is important to know not only *what* is being said but also *how* it is said. The entire meaning of a statement can change depending on whether the speaker says it in jest or in anger. How can the tone of a statement be conveyed in a technological environment that does not use live video or audio?

Clearly allied to the problem of no audio inflection is the lack of actually seeing the individual who makes a statement in the cyberclassroom. Professors' and students' facial expressions add meaning to a message. An arms-folded posture or a warm smile can communicate volumes. Facial

NEW DIRECTIONS FOR TEACHING AND LEARNING, no. 84, Winter 2000   © Jossey-Bass, a Wiley company

expressions and body language can contribute subtle (and sometimes not so subtle) meanings or attitudes (Bauman, 1997; Knapp & Hall, 1997; Levitt, 1964), but kinesthetics are lost in the online classroom.

However, the problem in online learning is more than the lack of audio and kinesthetic clues: the very environment of a classroom is nonexistent. Most of us remember professors and students from past classes. We remember their sense of humor (or lack of it). We are impressed with professors' preciseness or their disorganization. We remember students who worked hard on assignments and others who seemed uninterested and slept during class. For better or worse, proximity helps us connect with others. All of these interrelations have an influence on us, and some believe them to be an important part of the educational process (Bauman, 1997).

Because of the absence of audio and visual cues and the removal of the classroom environment, students often feel that they are alone. They feel that they are not communicating with other human beings; instead, they are communicating with hardware—piles of metal and circuits. At best, the perceived removal of humanity can lead to an antiseptic and boring learning environment. I even would argue that the removal of the human element creates an environment that is not conducive to maintaining ethical behavior among students. If the student does not see the pain of a hurtful remark, then it must not exist. If students do not understand that breaches of academic ethics (such as plagiarism or cheating) have "victims," then they are more likely to compromise the integrity of the online classroom.

The Solutions

The solution to the problems inherent in the cyberclassroom is to supply the elements normally found in the face-to-face classroom. In this section, I suggest six ways in which educators can humanize an online classroom.

Solution 1: Add Tone. Because written language does not supply auditory cues, professors of online courses should supply—and encourage students to supply—tone through the use of written cues. For example, if there is any question concerning the tone of a statement, it is appropriate for the author to make clear how a statement is to be understood: "I say this in jest." Or, "I am sorry to say."

Supplying tone through written body language and facial expressions can also make computer communication a more human experience. This requires more thought and effort than we are accustomed to in our daily conversation, but the effort will be rewarded by better communication.

One easy way to get participants to include body language is to encourage the use of well-known notations, such as emoticons. A smiley face : -) or a frown : - (can speak volumes about tone. A glossary of these notations could be supplied as part of the course for those who are unfamiliar with them. Many examples are more complicated than a simple smile.

: - &	tongue-tied
< : -)	the dunce
* : 0)	bozo
8 -)	wearing sunglasses

A more complete list of emoticons can be found at www.Newbie. netJumpStations/SmileyFAQ.html.

Emoticons should be used by writers to help express their meaning. They are not to be used to describe the tone of others; such usage would be dehumanizing.

Solution 2: Use Expressive Language. Often, students and professors in online courses write something and give little thought to how others interpret their words or little thought to the impression they are creating. If they were to consider how to communicate effectively with their audience, they would see that a vivid metaphor (Davitz & Mattis, 1964), an ironic twist, or even humorous hyperbole can enhance the expressiveness of their writing. As a result of more expressive writing, professors and students can better communicate their full engagement in a course. (For a discussion of how to evaluate students' written expression in an online course, see Article Nine.)

Solution 3: Create Biographies. To solve the problem of not having face-to-face contact with the professor and fellow students, the professor could supply biographical information and a photo. This could also be required of each student. The first assignment might be for each student to create a biography and post it to the course bulletin board. Information, such as hometown, previous schooling or experience, hobbies, educational goals, and future plans, can provide opportunities for students to see their similarities and appreciate classroom diversity.

A word of caution, however: students should not publish their home addresses or home phone numbers. Even though many software packages help the professor to password-protect a course Web site, sometimes the sites are compromised.

Solution 4: Create a Virtual Break Room. If students have hobbies or interests in common, they need a place to explore these similarities. In the traditional classroom, students can linger in the hallways after class to argue about who will win the various weekend sporting events, for example. Online students need similar opportunities to "hang out" and chat, outside the pressures of a formal classroom environment. Students must be able to talk with each other but escape a formal forum in which class discussion takes place with the guidance and input of the professor. More important, a virtual break room will provide opportunities for students to discuss the difficulties of a course informally. Not all such discussions should be within the purview of professors.

The details of how break rooms are created will depend on the technology being used. Some software offers built-in cyberlounges. When such software is not available, chat rooms and bulletin boards can be useful for casual conversation. (For an in-depth discussion on the definitions and advantages of synchronous and asynchronous delivery, see Article Three.)

Solution 5: Model Appropriate Interaction. Students should know that the professor is available and intellectually involved in the work of the course. Students should be aware of the professor's full participation in the interactions of the course, yet the professor must take care not to dominate the discussion. Appropriate participation on the part of the professor provides a model for appropriate interaction among students.

One way to model appropriate participation is to pay careful attention to details when communicating by computer. For example, one member of a discussion group in a course conducted using a listserv was offended by the repeated improper spelling of his name (Weiss & Morrison, 1998). This would be equivalent to mispronouncing a person's name repeatedly in class, which is something no one would want to do. This kind of faux pas can be dehumanizing.

In addition, learners need a classroom environment where they can feel free to experiment and to express themselves in appropriate ways. This means the environment needs to have a sense of safety and trust as well as openness. Giving well-conceived feedback to students is one way the professor demonstrates honesty. Another way the professor models honesty and trust is to communicate to each student a sense of goodwill and caring. Professors can accomplish this by offering an invitation for personal discussion and interaction. As one of my colleagues says in his online syllabus, "Drop me an e-mail about things in the course that interest you and confuse you. You never have to have an agenda to contact me. I'm here to help you."

Solution 6: Create an Ethical Community of Learners. Challenge the students to think about the ethics of online relationships (Palloff & Pratt, 1999). It is possible to challenge their ethical relativism in a way that will be educational (Speck, 1997). Students must understand that a breach in ethics has victims, that real people sit at the cyberdesk next to theirs.

Of course, freedom must exist within the online course, but freedom comes with ethical responsibilities. For example, because online courses require students to offer detailed explanations of their ideas, privacy may be an issue. Also, an atmosphere of acceptance will foster a sense of community. Students must understand that a spiteful reaction to a student's ideas—often called "a flame"—will burn when it is received. There will be open communication among students only if they are guaranteed that their ideas will be kept confidential and be accepted within the community of the online course. Such online course characteristics foster community.

Part of the process of building a sense of community often involves resolving group conflict and ethical breaches. The professor must help resolve the conflicts (Palloff & Pratt, 1999). Proactive resolution would involve an open discussion of how to respond to classmates' ideas in a meaningful and accepting way. Professors must teach students how to debate and discuss issues within an ethical framework.

Discussions about plagiarism also can help professors create an ethical community of learners. Sometimes students don't understand how to avoid plagiarism; other times, they resort to plagiarism because they do not have enough to say. To avoid both situations, students need collaboration (a strong sense of humanization). Not having enough to say is the result of isolation. A strong sense of community can help students connect with each other intellectually and feel that they are a community of learners bound by similar ethical responsibilities.

Conclusion

If an online course is handled in the proper way, the personality of the professor and camaraderie of fellow students can be achieved even in the absence of face-to-face contact. However, this will not happen automatically. The course must be taught in a way that cultivates relationships. If this is done, the professor and the students will be rewarded with a satisfying personal relationship despite the distance that separates them.

References

Bauman, M. (1997). *Online learning communities.* [http://leahi.kcc.hawaii.edu/org/tcc-conf97/pres/bauman.html].

Davitz, J., & Mattis, S. (1964). The communication of emotional meaning by metaphor. In J. Davitz (Ed.), *The communication of emotional meaning* (pp. 157–176). New York: McGraw-Hill.

Knapp, M., & Hall, J. (1997). *Nonverbal communication in human interaction.* Orlando: Harcourt Brace.

Levitt, E. (1964). The relationship between abilities to express emotional meanings vocally and facially. In J. Davitz (Ed.), *The communication of emotional meaning* (pp. 87–100). New York: McGraw-Hill.

Neal, E. (1998, June 19). Using technology in teaching: We need to exercise healthy skepticism. *Chronicle of Higher Education,* p. B4.

Palloff, R., & Pratt, K. (1999). *Building learning communicates in cyberspace: Effective strategies for the online classroom.* San Francisco: Jossey-Bass.

Speck, B. W. (1997). Challenging the validity of students' ethical relativism. *Perspectives,* 27(1), 55–70.

Weiss, R. E., & Morrison, G. R. (1998). Evaluation of a graduate seminar conducted by listserv. *Proceedings of Selected Paper Presentations at the Convention of the Association for Educational Communications and Technology* (pp. 463–478). Ames: Iowa State University.

RENÉE E. WEISS is the interim director of the Center for Academic Excellence at The University of Memphis in Memphis, Tennessee.

8

Professors need to create deep and durable learning in online classrooms. This article offers five principles to help them accomplish this goal.

Promoting Deep and Durable Learning in the Online Classroom

Douglas J. Hacker, Dale S. Niederhauser

If online classrooms are to replace or supplement traditional classrooms, then the responsibility falls to the advocates of online learning to ensure that pedagogically sound practice guides the design and use of online technologies. The question of whether even traditional classrooms manifest sound pedagogical practice notwithstanding, it would be remiss for advocates of online learning to promote it on the basis of expediency and not on quality. Therefore, in this article, we describe five principles of instruction that have been shown by empirical studies to promote deep and durable learning and then provide ways in which each of these principles can be embedded in the online classroom. We will stress ways in which the online classroom can be even more conducive than traditional classrooms to using these learning principles.

There are many learning principles from which to choose, but we narrow our focus to five that have particularly strong empirical support. First, effective instructors require students to become active participants in their own learning by asking them to construct deep explanations, justifications, and reasons for what they think and do. Second, learning is grounded in the effective use of examples. Third, collaborative problem solving increases not only specific problem-solving abilities but general metacognitive understanding of how, when, and why to use problem-solving strategies. Fourth, effective instruction uses feedback that is commensurate with performance (that is, neither too much nor too little feedback is provided to learners depending on their performance). Fifth, effective instruction has embedded within it motivational components that enhance self-efficacy and perceived challenge.

New Directions for Teaching and Learning, no. 84, Winter 2000   © Jossey-Bass, a Wiley company

Active Participants in Learning

Advocates of the current constructivist movement in education argue that instruction needs to promote a change in the role of students from passive recipients of knowledge to active constructors of their own knowledge (for example, Greeno, Collins, & Resnick, 1996; Mayer, 1996). Learners must be viewed as meaning makers who actively select, organize, and integrate their experiences with existing knowledge. Learners can be encouraged to become active constructors in many ways. One way is to require students to construct deep explanations, justifications, and reasons for what they think and do (Graesser, Person, & Magliano, 1995). "Interaction that consists of the mutual exchange of ideas, explanations, justifications, speculations, inferences, hypotheses, conclusions, and other high-level discussion promotes the construction of new knowledge" (King, 1997, p. 224).

To promote students' active construction of knowledge, professor-student and student-student interactions must be focused on deeper levels of understanding. This can be accomplished by requiring students to generate and verbalize their own explanations (Dominowski, 1998; King, 1997; Pressley, El-Dinary, & Brown, 1992). Acquiring new knowledge by articulating in one's own words how the new knowledge fits with existing knowledge has been shown to increase comprehension (King, 1994; Pressley, Wood, Woloshyn, Martin, King, & Menke, 1992).

A central feature of online classrooms is access to a variety of telecommunications tools. (See Article Three in this volume for more on this.) These tools provide opportunities for professor-student and student-student interactions to take many different forms that can promote active construction of knowledge through discussion. For example, e-mail can be used to develop individual question-response-clarification cycles between professor and students or among students. Deep questioning, with regular and timely responses, followed by clarifications of incomplete or erroneous knowledge, can promote high-quality and thoughtful e-mail interactions. E-mail discussions may actually produce more insightful discussion of ideas than face-to-face interactions because participants have the opportunity to frame, reflect on, and revise questions and responses before sending them (Harrington & Hathaway, 1994).

However, maintaining individual online question-response-clarification cycles with students can be extremely labor-intensive for professors, especially in classes with large enrollments. One way to lessen this burden on professors is to use group discussion forums like e-mail-based listservs or bulletin board–style newsgroups. A professor can send a single message—a question on an assigned reading, for example—to the listserv, and all students who are enrolled in that listserv will receive a copy. Student replies are also posted to the listserv so that all participants have access to the responses. Students then may choose to integrate peers' ideas into their responses by agreeing or disagreeing with the multiple perspectives rep-

resented. Thus, a discourse grows that does not depend on professor intervention. All participants take responsibility for the conversation as they
strive to explain their thoughts, develop and justify their ideas, and question each other to negotiate meaning within the listserv.

Newsgroups provide a more structured format that allows professor-
student and student-student discussion to be "threaded." This means that
replies are arranged hierarchically so that the reader can determine the
threads that run through a discussion. For example, a professor might pose
a question like this one: "How are issues of justice addressed in Hawthorne's
The Scarlet Letter?" One thread could be started with a student initiating a
discussion about legal interpretations of justice. Other students could
respond to this student and each other on this topic. Another student might
begin another thread on ethical justice, and students could respond within
this thread as well. The threading is represented graphically, so that readers
can track the threads of the discussion through the various issues that are
raised. Threaded discussions can be conducted on public newsgroups and
also have been incorporated into Web-based course development programs
like WebCT (Goldberg & Salari, 1997).

Asynchronous communication tools like listservs and newsgroups provide opportunities for students in online classrooms to engage in high-level
discussions by framing and presenting ideas, formulating challenging questions for peers, and responding to those questions to clarify misconceptions
that arise. Thus, students learn to develop reasoned responses that include
explanation and justification. Students also learn to devise and respond to
questions that require answers based on integration or synthesis of dispa-
rate chunks of knowledge, logical connections, and causal or goal-oriented
reasoning. Caution is warranted, however, because these forms of communication lack important features that are present in face-to-face interactions. (See Article Seven in this volume for more on personalizing
electronic communication.) Students may need explicit instruction to participate effectively in group-based, online communication forums. Developing supportive online communities can be promoted by establishing
guidelines for Internet etiquette, or "netiquette" (see McMurdo, 1995;
Scheuermann & Taylor, 1997).

Effective Use of Examples

The second learning principle—teaching through the use of examples—has
a history as long as instruction itself. The two dominant psychological paradigms of the twentieth century, behaviorism and cognitivism, continue to
place critical importance on the role examples can play in learning.
Although the two paradigms differ in how examples are used, the ultimate
goal of each is to enhance the generalizability or transfer of the critical elements learned in examples to new contexts. Behaviorists have argued for
the presentation of well-structured, positive, and negative examples that

focus on the critical common elements of concepts or skills (Butterfield & Nelson, 1989). Some cognitivists, however, argue for the use of contextualized and authentic anchored cases, that is, examples drawn from real-world experiences of students (see Brown, Collins, & Duguid, 1989; Vye, Schwartz, Bransford, Barron, Zech, & CTGV, 1998).

The behaviorally guided use of examples in computer-based instruction during the 1960s and 1970s met with limited success. However, recent work has shown that the use of examples that are anchored in contextualized and authentic cases can lead to improved educational outcomes (for example, Williams, 1992), and that case-based instruction may be well-suited to computer-based technologies (Anderson, Conrad, & Corbett, 1989; Vye et al., 1998). Anchoring instruction in specific real-world experiences promotes problem finding and solving, exploration, discovery, metacognitive processing of problem solving, and the transfer of learning (Vye et al., 1998).

Even though the use of case-based examples in distance education is relatively untested, general principles can guide their use (Graesser et al., 1995). Authentic cases (for example, determining the best way to spend $100 for a week's worth of groceries) are better than concrete cases (calculating how much rocket fuel is needed to get a two-ton payload into space), and concrete cases are better than symbolic cases (manipulating the variables in the equation $f = ma$). Regardless of the kind of case that is selected, beginning instruction should start with a case that is more generic or prototypical in nature to foster near transfer, but then should shift to cases that are more unusual to promote far transfer (Butterfield & Nelson, 1989). Cases that illustrate early learning skills should use simple simulations, and cases that illustrate advanced skills should use complex simulations (Bjork, 1994; Mayer & Sims, 1994). Finally, multiple cases with similar goals and that require similar processing should be used to increase perceived similarity among cases and increase transfer among them (Bjork, 1994).

Before using case-based examples in the online classroom, the professor must make decisions about selecting appropriate case formats, delivering the cases to students, and conducting case discussions with and among students. Once the professor has determined the type of case-based example to use (for example, an authentic prototypical case that illustrates early learning skills), an appropriate format can be chosen for presenting the case. For instance, some content can be presented using a written format. A growing number of case-based resource books are currently available (for example, Barnett, Goldstein, & Jackson, 1994; Shulman, 1992) that include written vignettes on a variety of topics across content areas. There is also evidence that video clips provide an effective format for case presentation (Richardson & Kyle, 1999). Video cases can be produced by videotaping specific examples of practice, or they may be purchased as stand-alone materials or as supplementary materials that accompany textbooks (for example, Eggen & Kauchak, 1999). Finally, computer software packages have been developed that include video case examples, which are integrated with activities and supporting materials (for example, Bowers, Barron, & Goldman, 1994; Goldman & Barron, 1990).

After the format for presenting the case has been selected, the online professor must decide how to deliver case examples to students. Text-based examples can be e-mailed to students or posted to a listserv or newsgroup. Students can download short video case examples or view video clips online. Although not all professors will have access to TV broadcast facilities, those who do could broadcast their case examples to remote sites. Finally, case-based videos or software can be assigned as a required text that students would purchase along with their other course texts and materials.

Discussing the issues and problems that are raised through a good case example is an essential component for promoting deep and durable learning from cases (Barnett, 1998; Harrington & Hathaway, 1994; Merseth, 1996). Case discussions can be conducted in the asynchronous formats described earlier. Students can be divided into small groups or participate in whole-class discussions. Newsgroups and other "threaded" discussion forums, like the bulletin board feature in WebCT online course development software (Goldberg & Salari, 1997), can be particularly effective in promoting rich and connected discussions because participants have time to read and reflect on their peers' ideas before posting their own messages (Harrington & Hathaway, 1994).

However, asynchronous formats also open the door to potential miscommunications. Because it is not just the words that carry meaning but how those words are spoken, it is sometimes difficult to recognize nuances like irony, sarcasm, or humor without seeing or hearing the actual speaker (again, see Article Seven in this volume). One way to address this problem is to conduct case discussions using desktop videoconferencing software like CU-SeeMe. This software allows participants at different sites to see, hear, and talk to each other using a computer, video camera, and Internet connection. The entire group can meet online, or if small groups are located at different sites, participants at each site can discuss issues with others at the site, then present their ideas to the larger group using videoconferencing technology.

Collaborative Problem Solving

Research on expert-novice collaboration and peer collaboration has shown that collaborative problem solving can increase specific problem-solving abilities and general metacognitive understanding of how, when, and why to use problem solving strategies (Daiute & Dalton, 1993; Greeno, 1991; Lave & Wenger, 1987). "During such interaction with another [collaboration], we clarify ideas, negotiate meaning, develop new skills, and construct new knowledge; thus, learning becomes a by-product of that interaction" (King, 1997, p. 221).

In order to foster collaboration, communications need to involve an interactive construction of knowledge between or among individuals rather than a simple taking of turns. Through mixed initiative dialogues, "meanings accumulate collaboratively and incrementally with ongoing repair" (Graesser et al., 1995, p. 367). Mixed initiative dialogues allow the learner to play a dual role. As speaker, the learner can articulate his or her understanding to the listener and receive feedback on that understanding; as listener, the learner judges the speaker's articulations against his or her understanding and provides feedback that either confirms or disconfirms the speaker's understanding.

The extent to which the distance education environment can support collaboration and mixed initiative dialogue depends, in part, on several key components that have been identified by Brown et al. (1989). First, the kinds of problems given to students must require collective problem solving. Presenting problems that could just as easily be solved by one person working alone as by a group working collaboratively will not only frustrate individual motivation but will undermine the collaborative process (Webb & Palincsar, 1996). Second, students must be provided with opportunities to understand the different roles needed to solve a particular problem and to reflect on how the different roles contribute to a solution. And third, efforts must be made to ensure that misconceptions and ineffective strategies are in fact being repaired through collaboration and mixed initiative dialogues.

The professor can design activities to provide collaborative problem-solving opportunities in the online classroom. For example, students can participate in developing and presenting group projects online. Information-sharing programs, such as CSILE (Scardamalia, Bereiter, Brett, Burtis, Calhoun, & Smith Lea, 1992; Scardamalia & Bereiter, 1996) and Lotus Notes (Kittner & Van Slyke, 1997), can be used to store student productions in one database to which all users have simultaneous access. Students can complete project-based assignments in which they select or are assigned different roles in gathering information and resources. They can then use communication software to work collaboratively and organize a project into a presentation for their peers or the professor. Presentations of projects can be made online using conferencing software like ClassPoint or NetMeeting.

Online educational research projects also provide opportunities for students to collaborate on the Web. Access Excellence (National Health Museum, 1999) provides a forum for participating in three types of online projects: collaborative projects, which facilitate the exchange of information and materials between classrooms; data collection projects for collecting and comparing data between classrooms; and research projects for developing and initiating an original research question in collaboration with research scientists. For example, a data collection project might involve students from across the United States in gathering and analyzing data on topics like acid rain or the strength of the sun's rays. Students collaborate to create a database that allows them to discern patterns in the national data that would not be possible if only local data were available.

Effective Use of Feedback

The fourth learning principle is that effective instruction uses feedback that is commensurate with performance. In their review of computer-aided instruction (CAI), Kluger and DeNisi (1996) conclude that CAI programs that provide feedback interventions to learners sometimes impair learning compared with programs that provide no feedback interventions. These authors explain that too much feedback may eventually serve as a crutch for the learner. Rather than learners using feedback that is generated from performing the actual task, they may come to rely on feedback generated from the CAI program to alert them to errors. Although it is important for learners to receive feedback to help reject erroneous performance, too much feedback may prevent them from learning how to regulate their performance on their own.

Researchers with instructional interests other than CAI also have come to the conclusion that withholding or reducing feedback in some cases may encourage greater learning (Bjork, 1994; VanLehn, 1990). Students need opportunities to discover their errors and repair them. Too much feedback given too soon can disrupt this discovery-and-repair process and lower student motivation to become self-directed learners (Graesser et al., 1995).

Furthermore, tailoring feedback to meet individual student needs is a difficult task, even in one-on-one tutoring (Person, Graesser, Magliano, & Kreuz, 1994), and may be more difficult in the distance education environment. Student isolation, inherent in the online classroom, makes giving effective feedback a central concern. Although students need to take responsibility for their own learning and become self-directed learners, they also need support, structure, and clarity from the professor.

Online professors can provide support systems through Web-course authoring systems like WebCT (Dabbagh & Schmitt, 1998). A detailed course calendar, syllabus, assignment list, and frequently asked questions (FAQ) section provide structure and information so students have complete information about the professor's expectations for the course. Students can be encouraged to seek peer feedback through discussion groups before contacting the professor with their questions. This encourages them to self-regulate their need for feedback and to access different sources of feedback rather than rely on a single authority. Professors can regularly monitor these discussion groups and participate when needed. If students are sharing misconceptions, or if the discussion is proceeding in unfruitful ways, the professor can intervene to provide constructive feedback. WebCT also provides an online grading sheet, allowing students to get feedback on their progress in the course at any time. A dedicated e-mail system within WebCT provides an important feedback loop between professor and students.

Motivational Components

The importance of motivation in learning cannot be overstated. Without motivation to learn, learning becomes a sterile process that is externally dictated and internally resisted. Therefore, effective instruction, regardless of the kind and context, must have within it motivational components that enhance self-efficacy and perceived challenges. Although the novelty of using technology per se may be motivating for some, steps may need to be taken to help others become motivated to engage in online learning. We believe that the previous four principles of instruction serve well not only as ways to enhance learning but also to enhance motivation to learn.

Requiring students to construct deep explanations, justifications, and reasons for what they think and do encourages them to become active participants in their own learning. The more active they become, the more willing they may be to engage in riskier and more challenging tasks, and when they are more willing to engage in riskier and more challenging tasks, the more self-efficacious they will become (Bandura, 1989). Self-efficacy, challenge, and motivation also can be encouraged by allowing students to select their own problems from a collection of problems (Lepper, Woolverton, Mumme, & Gurtner, 1993). Students could start with any problem from a collection of problems and determine their own path through the remaining problems.

Being involved in collaborative problem solving allows students to view their knowledge and skills in comparison with others (Daiute & Dalton, 1993). Therefore, collaborative problem solving provides students with opportunities to judge their subjective level of challenge on a task against how others perceive the challenge of the task. By reflecting on their own abilities against this backdrop of others' abilities, learners can gain a better understanding of their weaknesses and strengths. Knowing their strengths may motivate them to engage in problems that focus more precisely on their strengths.

Finally, in addition to providing neither too much nor too little feedback, the feedback that is provided could be designed to promote self-efficacy. Based on their analyses of expert human tutors, Lepper et al. (1993) have made three recommendations for enhancing student self-efficacy. First, professors should avoid direct negative feedback when telling students that they are wrong or that their efforts have not been fruitful. Instead, professors should guide students to the correct answer by providing hints and other more indirect feedback. Second, they should enhance students' successes through judicious use of praise for success. When praise is used, professors should be sure to note how difficult or atypical the successful problem solving was. Finally, professors should minimize failure by sharing responsibility for the failure or by indicating that the problem was unusually difficult.

Conclusion

A central question that we sought to answer in this article is whether deep and durable learning can occur in the online classroom. Although rigorous tests of the effectiveness of online classrooms have yet to be performed, we believe that providing pedagogically sound instruction online is already possible and has great potential to improve. The five principles of instruction that we have identified are a small but select group of principles that have received strong empirical support as being critical to learning. We have proposed practical ways in which these five principles can be embedded in online instruction.

However, we do not guarantee that these methods will lead to deep and durable learning. Learning will not necessarily occur just because a professor uses listservs, interactive video, information-sharing software packages, or desktop videoconferencing software. (See Article Eleven of this volume.) There is no substitute for reflective instructional practice, and it is up to the professor to reflect on whether students are learning and how they are expected to learn. There are great differences in the ways in which people construct knowledge, and there are equally large differences in the ways in which knowledge is constructed in different domains (Chi & Ceci, 1987). Some individuals may be well served by online delivery of instruction, but others may find online learning foreign.

Some of the ways in which online instruction can be delivered have great potential and may eventually prove to be more effective than traditional instruction. However, even if online classrooms only do just as well as traditional classrooms, advocates of online instruction have done their jobs. Still, an important question that continually must be kept in mind is whether the online classroom hinders learning. If the answer to this question is yes, then we must take a step back and seriously investigate what we are advocating.

References

Anderson, J. R., Conrad, F. G., & Corbett, A. T. (1989). Skill acquisition and the LISP tutor. *Cognitive Science, 13,* 467–505.

Bandura, A. (1989). Human agency in social cognitive theory. *American Psychologist, 44,* 1175–1184.

Barnett, C. (1998). Mathematics teaching cases as a catalyst for informed strategic inquiry. *Teaching and Professor Education, 14,* 81–93.

Barnett, C., Goldstein, D., & Jackson, B. (Eds.) (1994). *Mathematics teaching cases: Fractions, decimals, ratios, and percentages.* Portsmouth, NH: Heinemann.

Bjork, R. A. (1994). Memory and metamemory considerations in the training of human beings. In J. Metcalfe & A. P. Shimamura (Eds.), *Metacognition: Knowing about knowing* (pp. 185–205). Cambridge, MA: MIT Press.

Bowers, J., Barron, L., & Goldman, E. (1994). An interactive media environment to enhance mathematics professor education. In J. Willis, B. Robin, & D. A. Willis (Eds.), *Technology and professor education annual* (pp. 515–519). Charlottesville, VA: Association for the Advancement of Computing in Education.

Brown, J. S., Collins, A., & Duguid, P. (1989). Situated cognition and the culture of learning. *Educational Researcher, 18,* 32–42.

Butterfield, E. C., & Nelson, G. D. (1989). Theory and practice of teaching for transfer. *Educational Technology Review & Development, 37,* 5–38.

Chi, M.T.H., & Ceci, S. J. (1987). Content knowledge: Its role, representation, and restructuring in memory development. In H. W. Reese (Ed.), *Advances in child development and behavior* (pp. 91–142). Orlando: Academic Press.

Dabbagh, N. H., & Schmitt, J. (1998). Redesigning instruction through web-based course authoring tools. *Educational Media International, 35,* 106–110.

Daiute, C., & Dalton, B. (1993). Collaboration between children learning to write: Can novices be masters? *Cognition and Instruction, 10,* 281–333.

Dominowski, R. L. (1998). Verbalization and problem solving. In D. J. Hacker, J. Dunlosky, & A. C. Graesser (Eds.), *Metacognition in educational theory and practice* (pp. 25–46). Hillsdale, NJ: Erlbaum.

Eggen, P., & Kauchak, D. (1999). *Educational psychology: Windows on classrooms* (4th ed.). Upper Saddle River, NJ: Merrill.

Goldberg, M. W., & Salari, S. (1997, June). An update on WebCT (World-Wide-Web Course Tools)—A tool for the creation of sophisticated Web-based learning environments. *Proceedings of NAUWeb '97—Current Practices in Web-Based Course Development.* Flagstaff: Northern Arizona University.

Goldman, E., & Barron, L. (1990). Using hypermedia to improve the preparation of elementary professors. *Journal of Professor Education, 41,* 21–31.

Graesser, A. C., Person, N. K., & Magliano, J. P. (1995). Collaborative dialogue patterns in naturalistic one-to-one tutoring. *Applied Cognitive Psychology, 9,* 359–387.

Greeno, J. G. (1991). Number sense as situated knowing in a conceptual domain. *Journal for Research in Mathematics Teaching, 22,* 170–218.

Greeno, J. G., Collins, A. M., & Resnick, L. B. (1996). Cognition and learning. In D. C. Berliner & R. C. Calfee (Eds.), *Handbook of educational psychology* (pp. 15–46). New York: Simon & Schuster Macmillan.

Harrington, H. L., & Hathaway, R. S. (1994). Computer conferencing, critical reflection, and professor development. *Teaching and Professor Education, 10,* 543–554.

King, A. (1994). Guiding knowledge construction in the classroom: Effects of teaching children how to question and how to explain. *American Educational Research Journal, 31,* 338–368.

King, A. (1997). ASK to THINK-TEL WHY: A model of transactive peer tutoring for scaffolding higher level complex thinking. *Educational Psychologist, 32,* 221–235.

Kittner, M., & Van Slyke, C. (1997, December). *An innovative approach to teaching decisions support systems.* Paper presented at the International Academy for Information Management Annual Conference, Atlanta.

Kluger, A. N., & DeNisi, A. (1996). The effects of feedback interventions on performance: A historical review, a meta-analysis, and a preliminary feedback intervention theory. *Psychological Bulletin, 119,* 254–284.

Lave, J., & Wenger, E. (1987). *Situated learning: Legitimate peripheral participation.* Cambridge: Cambridge University Press.

Lepper, M. R., Woolverton, M., Mumme, D. L., & Gurtner, J.-L. (1993). Motivational techniques of expert human tutors: Lessons for the design of computer-based tutors. In S. P. Lajoie & S. J. Derry (Eds.), *Computers as cognitive tools* (pp. 75–105). Hillsdale, NJ: Erlbaum.

Mayer, R. E. (1996). Learners as information processors: Legacies and limitations of educational psychology's second metaphor. *Educational Psychologist, 31,* 151–161.

Mayer, R. E., & Sims, V. K. (1994). For whom is a picture worth a thousand words? Extensions of a dual-coding theory of multimedia learning. *Journal of Educational Psychology, 86,* 389–401.

McMurdo, G. (1995). Netiquettes for networkers. *Journal of Information Science, 21,* 305–318.

Merseth, K. K. (1996). Cases and the case method in professor education. In J. Sikula (Ed.), *Handbook of research on professor education* (pp. 722–746). New York: Macmillan.

National Health Museum (1999). *Access excellence.* [www.accessexcellence.org.].

Person, N. K., Graesser, A. C., Magliano, J. P., & Kreuz, R. J. (1994). Inferring what the student knows in one-to-one tutoring: The role of student questions and answers. *Learning and Individual Differences, 6,* 205–229.

Pressley, M., El-Dinary, P. B., & Brown, R. (1992). Skilled and not-so-skilled reading: Good information processing and not-so-good information processing. In M. Pressley, K. R. Harris, & J. T. Guthrie (Eds.), *Promoting academic competence and literacy in school* (pp. 91–127). Orlando: Academic Press.

Pressley, M., Wood, E., Woloshyn, V. E., Martin, V., King, A., & Menke, D. (1992). Encouraging mindful use of prior knowledge: Attempting to construct explanatory answer facilitates learning. *Educational Psychologist, 27,* 91–109.

Richardson, V., & Kyle, R. S. (1999). Learning from videocases. In M. Lundeberg, B. Levin, & H. Harrington (Eds.), *Who learns what from cases and how?* Hillsdale, NJ: Erlbaum.

Scardamalia, M., & Bereiter, C. (1996). Engaging students in a knowledge society. *Educational Leadership, 54,* 6–10.

Scardamalia, M., Bereiter, C., Brett, C., Burtis, P. J., Calhoun, C., & Smith Lea, N. (1992). Educational applications of a networked communal database. *Interactive Learning Environments, 2,* 45–71.

Scheuermann, L., & Taylor, G. (1997). Netiquette. *Internet Research, 7,* 269–273.

Shulman, J. H. (Ed.). (1992). *Case methods in professor education.* New York: Professors College Press.

VanLehn, K. (1990). *Mind bugs: The origins of procedural misconceptions.* Cambridge, MA: MIT Press.

Vye, N. J., Schwartz, D. L., Bransford, J. D., Barron, B. J., Zech, L., & Cognition and Technology Group at Vanderbilt (1998). SMART environments that support monitoring, reflection, and revision. In D. J. Hacker, J. Dunlosky, & A. C. Graesser (Eds.), *Metacognition in educational theory and practice* (pp. 305–346). Hillsdale, NJ: Erlbaum.

Webb, N. M., & Palincsar, A. S. (1996). Group processes in the classroom. In D. C. Berliner & R. C. Calfee (Eds.), *Handbook of educational psychology* (pp. 841–873). New York: Simon & Schuster Macmillan.

Williams, S. M. (1992). Putting case-based instruction into context: Examples from legal and medical education. *Journal of Learning Sciences, 2,* 367–427.

DOUGLAS J. HACKER *is an assistant professor in the Department of Educational Studies at the University of Utah in Salt Lake City.*

DALE S. NIEDERHAUSER *is an assistant professor in the Department of Educational Studies and the director of Distance Education for the University of Utah Reading Center in Salt Lake City.*

9

*Professors can use a three-part rubric for evaluating
students' written work in online classrooms, and an
electronic portfolio can be a valuable summative
assessment tool in the online course.*

Evaluating Students'
Written Performance
in the Online Classroom

John F. Bauer, Rebecca S. Anderson

Computer technology is creating a subtle but dynamic shift in teaching
methods. The rapidly falling student-to-computer ratio in today's classrooms
provides ample evidence of an inexorable movement toward computer-
oriented lessons. The shift is most noticeable in higher education, where
print has begun to move from paper to screen as professors require work to
be submitted on floppy disks or sent via e-mail. In many classes, for example, essays are written with word processing, attached to e-mail, and sent to
professors who open them, evaluate them, and send them back. On a
broader front, entire courses and degree programs are offered as part of distance learning.

Because more classes are going online, there are significant changes in
educational measurement methodology (Ross & Morrison, 1995). Class
attendance as an assessment tool becomes extinct, whereas class participation becomes quantifiable. Verbally acrobatic students in traditional classrooms are forced in online classrooms to showcase their wares in print to
maintain their preeminence. How to assess students' writing is a major concern for both professors and students.

We understand that online classes can be taught and assessed using the
traditional teacher-centered behavioral model, with objective testing as the
basis for both formative and summative evaluation. Because evaluation techniques for this model do not necessitate reinvention, we focus our discussion on the more contemporary constructivist model. By this we mean that
the professor acts as a facilitator, expects a high degree of individual participation, and assigns group projects that stimulate the cognitive processes

NEW DIRECTIONS FOR TEACHING AND LEARNING, no. 84, Winter 2000   © Jossey-Bass, a Wiley company

and are initiated and controlled by learners (Jonassen, 1995). (See Article One in this volume for a discussion of the constructivist model.) The purpose of this article is to discuss the design of a rubric for grading online student work produced from a constructivist paradigm and to provide suggestions for those interested in using an electronic portfolio (e-folio) as an assessment vehicle.

Establishing Criteria for a Rubric

To ensure meaningful and fair assessment, professors should make students thoroughly familiar with how their work will be judged (Speck, 1998). Without the luxury of class time to launch into verbal explanations or to float tangential examples of expectations, professors will need to construct and explain expectations as precisely as possible the first time around (Hobson, 1998). The need to construct and explain expectations not only applies to formal writing assignments but also to the content of general discussion. The informal discussion responses of students that used to be a vague part of the professor's memory of the regular classroom can become a permanent record in a database and therefore accessible again and again. This "replayability" factor (Sheingold & Fredericksen, 1994) allows professors to grade informal discussions. Lowry, Koneman, Osman-Jouchoux, and Wilson (1994) provide a case of the replayability factor when content analysis of an early e-mail class revealed a fair amount of "unrelated discourse," jokes, and chitchat among group members.

In assessing students' writing—both informal and formal—in the online classroom, it is best if both teacher and student internalize standards, so that writing toward those standards becomes instinctual (Taylor, 1996). With a clearer understanding of the expectations, students are likely to learn more from the tasks (Anderson, 1998). Moreover, with clear criteria to guide them, students can more effectively evaluate their own writing.

We suggest four major components for an online assessment rubric that will help professors evaluate both formal writing and informal written discussions. In particular, we focus on three major aspects of writing: *content, expression,* and *participation.*

Content. Evaluating the content of student written work has always been difficult because it remains least quantifiable. Thus, a rubric evaluating content should connect professors' judgments with numerical equivalents (Morrison & Ross, 1998). Exhibit 9.1 provides an example of a rubric that makes this connection.

If content is the most difficult to assess, it is often scored at a higher percentage of the total grade because it gives direct and continual evidence of critical thinking and argumentation skills (Marttunen, 1998). For instance, a student who posts an astute analysis (critical thinking) gives evidence of an obvious grasp of the topic (content).

Exhibit 9.1. Rubric for Online Content Assessment

Number of Points	Skills
9–10	Demonstrates excellence in grasping key concepts; critiques the work of others; provides ample evidence of support for opinions; readily offers new interpretations of discussion material.
7–8	Shows evidence of understanding most of the major concepts; is able to agree or disagree when prompted; is skilled in basic level of support for opinions; offers an occasional divergent viewpoint.
5–6	Has mostly shallow grasp of the material; rarely takes a stand on issues; offers inadequate levels of support.
1–4	Shows no significant understanding of material.

Expression. Expression gives clarity to content. The best ideas lie fallow if they are not expressed well. Good writing is synonymous with good scholarship and must be accorded a high place in assessment. Numerical assessments are sometimes held in disdain (Bean & Peterson, 1998). Nonetheless, a rubric with an attendant point system can provide students with a clearly identifiable scale for measuring their expression (see Exhibit 9.2). A point system also gives professors some leverage, say, when it is clear that a run-on sentence or a fragment has muddied the waters of content. Conversely, students who write with a measure of sophistication can be given credit even if their responses are off the mark.

The online class poses a peculiar difficulty in evaluating expression. Common verbal transgressions that go overlooked in normal class discussions become permanent artifacts in the online classroom. A suggestion, then, is to divide the expression rubric into two categories: formal postings and projects where language usage will be assessed, and online discussions, with the emphasis on content and participation. The second of these two categories is important because students need to develop their sense of spontaneous debate and discussion. If professors tell students that they will scrutinize the construction of every thought produced on the screen, they run the risk of being counterproductive, especially in terms of participation. It is important for professors to replicate what will be tolerated in a live class discussion, where it would be rare for an occasional mispronounced word, a fragmented utterance, or use of the vernacular to be corrected on the spot.

Participation. Online classes usually call for postings to plenary e-mail discussions, listservs, and bulletin board systems, and professors will want to determine how to evaluate student participation in such settings. In addition, in the confines of small-group projects, professors may want to assess whether group members participate in equal shares. Grading the

Exhibit 9.2. Rubric for Assessing Expression in Formal Online Postings

Number of Points	Skills
9–10	Student uses complex, grammatically correct sentences on a regular basis; expresses ideas clearly, concisely, cogently, in logical fashion; uses words that demonstrate a high level of vocabulary; has rare misspellings.
7–8	Sentences are generally grammatically correct; ideas are readily understood but show signs of disorganization; some transitions between concepts are missing; there are occasional misspellings, especially with homonyms not detected with spelling checks.
5–6	Poor use of the language garbles much of the message; only an occasional idea surfaces clearly; language is disjointed; there is overuse of the simple sentence and repetition of words; paragraphs are often unrelated to each other.
1–4	Writing is largely unintelligible.

participation of students in small groups may head off the common lament, "I had to do this all by myself, because no one else helped." Students quickly realize that the online classroom provides the teacher a greater opportunity to analyze responses than do the face-to-face discussions of the regular class (Weiss & Morrison, 1998).

A rubric for participation might be easier to develop than those for content and expression. Simple math can determine if students are participating in equal shares. But why is quantity of writing worthy of evaluation? First, quantity is important because students need to use writing regularly as a way to think on paper and thus discover what there is to say about a particular topic. Such discovery writing often requires a good dose of writing. Second, when students produce significant amounts of writing so that the professor can interact with them about the writing, the professor can begin to develop a relationship of trust with students. As Berge (1997) notes, a sense of trust between professor and student is a central element in the learner-centered approach. Assessing adequate and timely participation can determine if students are earning this trust. Third, when professors evaluate students for the quantity of the writing, pathologically quiet types often come alive (Bean & Peterson, 1998). Those who aren't comfortable speaking in front of a live audience will tap with abandon at the keyboard. Online postings neutralize those who are quick on their feet and give the reticent an equal chance to help discussions flourish. Exhibit 9.3 is a model for assessing the quantity of students' online participation.

Exhibit 9.3. Rubric for Assessing Online Participation

Number of Points	Skills
9–10	Contributions are prompt, timely, relevant, self-initiated; remarks are posted freely on all assignments throughout the course; there is no attempt to dominate conversation.
7–8	Student generally keeps up with the discussion; needs an occasional prompting to contribute; might participate in some discussions more than others.
5–6	Participation is spotty; picks and chooses topics to get involved in; offers short, perfunctory postings when prompted; takes limited initiative.
1–4	Student rarely participates freely; makes short, irrelevant remarks.

Electronic Portfolios

Another way to assess students' online writing is through an e-folio, Web-folio, or digital portfolio. This type of online assessment serves the student as an instrument of reflection and analysis and serves the professor as an evaluation tool that integrates student evaluations (Mullin, 1998).

To make the e-folio work, professors should advise students of its worth as a final product and explain what should be included in it. The e-folio rubric must ultimately specify the types of documents (called artifacts) that will be included, the number of artifacts, and the point scale for judging each artifact. (Exhibit 9.4 provides a sample rubric.) Wiedmer (1998) identifies three kinds of rubrics for the e-folio: the analytic, whereby each section of the e-folio is graded on an individual scale; the holistic, in which the e-folio is judged in its entirety, without breaking it into parts; the primary trait, which assesses the performance in one or more major areas of emphasis.

Regardless of the type of rubric used, e-folios should require peer and self-evaluation. For example, students may be asked to submit written reflections about their artifacts, explanations of how they met course objectives, and discussions of what they learned in the course. Other items for this category include student evaluation of message content, form, style, and tone (Knupfer, Gram, & Larson, 1997). Where group projects are concerned, comments devoted to critiquing the work of others and the quality of peer relationships developed online may be valuable.

Grading the e-folio is remarkably different from grading traditional portfolios. What will be missing is the beauty of colorful pages and the snazzy, glitzy three-ringed binders. But these adornments will be replaced by clip art from the Web in the new cut, paste, and send style. Letting students run with their electronic imaginations can yield intriguing results. For

Exhibit 9.4. Rubric for Assessing the E-Folio

Number of Points	Skills
9–10	Meets or exceeds required quantity of artifacts; artifacts are creatively presented and well organized; shows significant level of meaningful reflection; provides strong evidence of peer and self-assessment; show an obvious investment of time and effort.
7–8	Meets required quantity of artifacts; shows some creativity and adequate organization; demonstrates some amount of meaningful reflection; includes evidence of peer and self-assessment; generally shows a good effort.
5–6	Less than the required number of artifacts; lacks creativity; shows little reflection on items; offers some peer and self-assessment; shows a limited effort.
1–4	Shows a poor effort to meet any of the requirements.

Source: Adapted from Scanlon & Ford, 1998.

example, McKinney (1998) reports that the sound and movement functions available to process a portfolio enabled one student the chance to use the musical theme from "The Twilight Zone" to announce to the reader, "You are about to enter the portfolio zone."

Conclusion

The class taught entirely online will become commonplace in higher education. Thus, effective evaluation in the online classroom will be a primary issue. When online material is submitted, and when it becomes an important student-centered activity and requirement of the class, we recommend judging the students' content, expression, and participation. These three criteria can provide a unique perspective from which to view students' formal writings and informal discussions. At the end of a course, an e-folio can offer students a chance to reflect on their own work and thus become more involved in the assessment process.

References

Anderson, R. S. (1998). Why talk about different ways to grade? The shift from traditional assessment to alternative assessment. In R. S. Anderson & B. W. Speck (Eds.), *Changing the way we grade student performance: Classroom assessment and the new learning paradigm* (pp. 5–16). San Francisco: Jossey-Bass.

Bean, J. C., & Peterson, D. (1998). Grading classroom participation. In R. S. Anderson & B. W. Speck (Eds.), *Changing the way we grade student performance: Classroom assessment and the new learning paradigm* (pp. 33–40). San Francisco: Jossey-Bass.

Berge, Z. (1997). Characteristics of online teaching in post-secondary, formal education. *Educational Technology, 37,* 35–47.

Hobson, E. H. (1998). Designing and grading written assignments. In R. S. Anderson & B. W. Speck (Eds.), *Changing the way we grade student performance: Classroom assessment and the new learning paradigm* (pp. 51–57). San Francisco: Jossey-Bass.

Jonassen, D. H. (1995, July-August). Supporting communities of learners with technology: A vision for integrating technology with learning in schools. *Education Technology*, pp. 60–63.

Knupfer, N. N., Gram, T. E., & Larsen, E. Z. (1997). Participant analysis of a multi-class, multi-state, on-line, discussion list. *Proceedings of Selected Research and Development Presentations at the 1997 National Convention of the Association for Educational Communication and Technology*. (ED 409845) Ames: Iowa State University.

Lowry, M., Koneman, P., Osman-Jouchoux, R., & Wilson, B. (1994, March). Electronic discussion groups. Using e-mail as an instructional strategy. *Tech Trends*, pp. 22–24.

Marttunen, M. (1998). Electronic mail as a forum for argumentative interaction in higher education studies. *Journal of Educational Computing Research, 18*(4), 397–405.

McKinney, M. (1998, Winter). Preservice teachers' electronic portfolios: Integrating technology, self-assessment, and reflection. *Teacher Education Quarterly*, pp. 85–103.

Morrison, G. R., & Ross, S. M. (1998). Evaluating technology-based processes and products. In R. S. Anderson & B. W. Speck (Eds.), *Changing the way we grade student performance: Classroom assessment and the new learning paradigm* (pp. 69–77). San Francisco: Jossey-Bass.

Mullin, J. A. (1998). Portfolios: Purposeful collections of student work. In R. S. Anderson & B. W. Speck (Eds.), *Changing the way we grade student performance: Classroom assessment and the new learning paradigm* (pp. 79–87). San Francisco: Jossey-Bass.

Ross, S., & Morrison, G. (1995). Evaluation as a tool for research and development: Issues and trends in its application to instructional technology. In R. D. Tennyson & A. E. Barron (Eds.), *Automating instructional design: Computer-based development and delivery tools*. New York: Springer Verlag.

Scanlon, P. A., & Ford, M. P. (1998). Grading student performance in real-world settings. In R. S. Anderson & B. W. Speck (Eds.), *Changing the way we grade student performance: Classroom assessment and the new learning paradigm* (pp. 97–105). San Francisco: Jossey-Bass.

Sheingold, K., & Fredericksen, J. (1994). Using technology to support innovative assessment. In B. Means (Ed.), *Technology and educational reform* (pp. 111–131). San Francisco: Jossey-Bass.

Speck, B. W. (1998). Unveiling some of the mystery of professional judgment in classroom assessment. In R. S. Anderson & B. W. Speck (Eds.), *Changing the way we grade student performance: Classroom assessment and the new learning paradigm* (pp. 17–31). San Francisco: Jossey-Bass.

Taylor, C. T. (1994). Assessment for the measurement of standards: The peril and promise of large-scale assessment reform. *American Education Research Journal, 31*, 231–262.

Weiss, R. E., & Morrison, G. R. (1998). Evaluation of a graduate seminar conducted by listserv. *Proceedings of Selected Paper Presentations at the Convention of the Association for Educational Communications and Technology* (pp. 463–478). Ames: Iowa State University.

Wiedmer, T. L. (1998). Digital portfolios: Capturing and demonstrating skills and levels of performance. *Phi Delta Kappan, 79*(8), 586–589.

JOHN F. BAUER *is a doctoral student in the Department of Instruction and Curriculum Leadership at The University of Memphis in Memphis, Tennessee.*

REBECCA S. ANDERSON *is the director of Writing Across the Curriculum for The University of Memphis (in Memphis, Tennessee) and an associate professor in the Department of Instruction and Curriculum Leadership.*

10

This article puts forward three criticisms of the academy's relationship to online teaching and makes recommendations for correcting the underlying problems at issue.

The Academy, Online Classes, and the Breach in Ethics

Bruce W. Speck

When I first thought about writing this article, my purpose was to discuss the ethics of teaching online courses. I was interested in the ethics of classroom teaching and found literature about that topic informative (Audi, 1994; Cahn, 1990; Fisch, 1996; Kidder, 1995). However, the more I read about the digital reform of higher education, the more I realized that the ethics of teaching had been compromised by commercialization. Thus, I saw that discussing the entrenched problem of plagiarism, for instance, even in online classes, and presenting solutions to that problem (for example, www.plagiarism.org; Ryan, 1999) did not take precedence over investigating the ethical breach in the educational contract that the academy is marketing at present. Therefore, my purpose here is to provide information that questions whether online classes in principle and in fact achieve the primary goal of education.

To address the ethical breach in the educational contract, I offer three criticisms. The first is that the academy has failed to conduct a thorough investigation of the efficacy of learning in online classrooms. The second is that concomitantly the academy has failed to prepare professors to teach online classes. The third is that the academy has adopted the entrepreneurial impulse for economic gain—an impulse that overrides the integrity of the academic mission.

In each of these I am criticizing the academy, not individual institutions. Although some institutions may not have betrayed the ethical conduct that the academy has historically expected of its citizens, and indeed, may have honored that conduct in addressing the viability of online classes, my concern is with the academy as a whole, and my criticisms address a trend that cuts across institutions, whatever their Carnegie status. Because the academy is engaged in an undertaking with ethical implications, I also suggest ways to redress the current breach in ethics.

Criticism One

The academy has failed to conduct a thorough investigation of the efficacy of learning in online classrooms. It should be noted that my criticism is not that the academy has not conducted some sort of research into online classes. The literature I cite in this article is evidence that the academy has conducted research into online classes. The articles in this volume are evidence that the academy is engaged in conducting (and citing) research about the educational usefulness of online classes. My claim is that the academy is engaging in marketing online classes without having conducted anything approaching *sufficient* research to determine whether online classes do, indeed, make good on the promise of effective teaching and its corollary, effective learning. Whether online classes can in principle and do in fact achieve the primary goal of education can be determined only on the basis of solid research and established learning theories. In short, solid, extensive research is foundational to the academic enterprise, and I accuse the academy of betraying this central tenet of academic life in its headlong pursuit of creating and marketing online courses.

Perhaps the most telling bit of research is that done by Merisotis and Phipps (1999). They conducted a metanalysis of research on distance learning and found that such research "does not include a theoretical or conceptual framework" (p. 15). Such research not only is bereft of a theoretical framework but is in other ways deeply flawed. For instance, after reviewing research literature purporting to show that distance education works, Merisotis and Phipps conclude, "The overall quality of the original research is questionable and thereby renders many of the findings inconclusive" (p. 14). By their estimate, "The research on distance learning has a long way to go" (p. 17).

I am not decrying the efforts of the academy to conduct research on online classes; rather, I applaud such efforts, and given the testimony of Merisotis and Phipps, we need to develop a body of research that thoroughly investigates online classes and other forms of distance education. We should continue to push ahead in our efforts to determine whether online courses are effective learning environments. My complaint is that the academy is experimenting with online classes on a large scale without the research evidence needed to support claims that online classes are indeed effective in promoting learning. As Ehrmann (1999) says, "All of us wish we had good data about teaching, learning, and technology, but few institutions are doing the work to get it. That's dangerous. Technology changes quickly and unpredictably, IT budgets are large and getting larger, and money remains tight. Lacking data, faculty and administrators make big investments of time and money with their eyes closed" (p. 25).

Green (1999) also notes, "Information technology has yet to transform classrooms, the instructional activities of most faculty, or the learning experiences of most students. Moreover, while we know that technology changes the learning experience, we do not have hard, consistent evidence documenting that it enhances academic achievement and learning outcomes" (p. 13). Green is referring to information technology broadly and not specifically to the online classroom, which presents even greater challenges; in the online classroom the professor and students "see" each other only through the typed words they exchange.

We might take heart when Green says that "virtually all schools and colleges are still in the early stages of adopting various kinds of IT resources into their instructional functions" (p. 13), if it were not for the fact that the academy is using the results of early experimentation that lacks theoretical rigor to promote online classes. In fact, the jury is still out on the efficacy of online classes to promote learning.

What may be even more damning is that, as Carstens and Worsfold point out in Article Eleven of this volume, the electronic classroom may be a place that does not promote learning—may even be a place that keeps people from learning. The literature Carstens and Worsfold cite is not published in obscure places, so it is readily available to the academy. Is the problem, then, that the academy is not willing to conduct a thorough investigation of online courses because such a research agenda would obstruct other objectives? In addition, although Hacker and Niederhauser, in Article Eight of this volume, promote online classes, they raise the question of whether such classes hinder learning. In responding to their own question, they say, "If the answer to this question is yes, then we must take a step back and seriously investigate what we are advocating" (p. 61).

At present, the academy does not have an adequate research base to justify the proliferation of online classes, and the research that has been conducted cannot in good faith support the widespread teaching and proliferation of those classes. Yet all of this seems to have little bearing on the academy's rush to become wired—a rush, I reiterate, that appears to be heedless of the ethical fabric of academic life.

Criticism Two

Concomitantly, the academy has failed to prepare professors to teach online classes. If the first criticism is cogent, the second follows logically: if the academy does not have adequate research to demonstrate that online classes do indeed promote effective learning, then the academy would be in the dark about how to train professors to teach such classes. But for the sake of exploration, let's assume that the academy has quality research to demonstrate that online classes do promote learning. Is the academy translating the fruits of quality research into effective teaching strategies? The answer is no. As Feenberg (1999) observes, "Universities do not seem anxious to make the enormous expenditures on adaptation and training that typically accompany the acquisition of complex new computer systems in the business world" (p. 5).

This should come as no surprise to those familiar with the continuing education philosophy of higher education: the doctorate is the prerequisite for tenure-track positions (in most cases) and faculty, by virtue of their academic training, have the finely honed ability to continue their education by reading, delivering conference papers, publishing their work, and translating all of these efforts at self-education into palatable learning experiences for their students.

This model of a professor's self-education continues to dominate the academy's notion of how a graduate student prepares to become a professor and, after securing a professorial position, develops as a professor. The model predicts that professors who, for whatever reason, gain an interest in using technology in their teaching will learn how to use technology effectively in their classroom. The model therefore assumes a learning process driven by individual initiative, needing little institutional support other than institutional provisions of hardware and software. (Indeed, in some cases, the motivated professor cannot depend on the institution to provide adequate hardware and software and therefore either seeks external support for those items or digs into his or her pocket to provide the resources.)

My purpose here is neither to defend nor to criticize this traditional model of faculty development. Rather, my purpose is to note that the academy has deviated from this model. The academy recognizes that the model assumed the linkage of professorial expertise in subject matter content with expertise in pedagogy. In an attempt to repair that faulty assumption, the academy has funded teaching and learning centers, sought to provide graduate students with pedagogical training as preparation for tenure-track positions, and promoted writing-across-the-curriculum programs. Thus, the academy has admitted—sometimes grudgingly—that professors need pedagogical training to deliver subject matter content effectively.

Yet this newfound conviction that faculty need training in pedagogy is conveniently disregarded when online courses are in view. The academy not only fails to provide adequate training for professors to teach online courses but also undermines professorial authority by putting them in situations where they are dependent on others to deliver subject matter content. This dependence is not merely a matter of supporting professorial intentions in the online classroom but of shaping those intentions by the imposition of technology. It does not matter whether professors want to use chat rooms, for instance. They *must* use chat rooms. To question the utility of e-mail as a useful pedagogical device, as another example, is to identify oneself as a cyberphilistine. In other words, the academy calls into question the professor's ability to make critical judgments about the relationship between content and pedagogy without providing adequate research (Criticism One) or the training (Criticism Two) to support them as they attempt to use technology to teach subject matter. In doing this, the academy violates the contract it has with students—namely, the agreement that professors are credentialed as expert teachers. Thus, the academy nullifies its own authority by its unethical practice of undermining the integrity of professorial judgment, the very judgment that is the basis for the educational contract between the academy and students.

The academy's promises—explicit and implicit—to provide students with an education are based at least in part on the fact that professors have the requisite expertise. The traditional faculty development model assumed that professors were credentialed experts by virtue of their graduate training. Thus, the academy entered into a contract with students promising that for so many dollars, a student could attend classes and, with reasonable effort, could expect to receive an education. Professorial expertise, therefore, was the basis for the academy's contractual agreement with students. Yet the academy has called into question the validity of linking subject matter expertise with teaching expertise as assumed by the traditional model and has thereby called into question its contract with students. At the same time, the academy continues to promote a contract based on assurances that professorial expertise is intact, when it is not providing the training *it deems essential* to support contractual obligations.

Although I have made a distinction between the academy and professors, such a distinction is tenuous. In many cases, professors either have jumped on the online bandwagon or tacitly demurred, either hoping retirement will deliver them from the fray or pursuing their own careers while keeping a wary eye on the pedagogy-technology nexus in the academy. But I need to be more generous. The digital reform of the academy has happened so quickly and with such little consultation with faculty that the "transformation" of higher education is being conducted without due regard for faculty expertise, either in conducting research to determine the efficacy of online courses or in developing information about how to teach effectively in online courses, should they be shown to be effective means of teaching students.

Whether the traditional faculty development model is adequate to ensure that professors are prepared to teach effectively in online classes is a matter for greater consideration. However, a core ideal that undergirds the model—namely, integrity of professorial judgment—is under attack. For instance, Daniel (1997) opposes a "laissez-faire approach" to developing and teaching online classes and is opposed to "letting individual faculty members or their departments do their own thing" (p. 16). According to Daniel, the laissez-faire approach won't work when the academy considers effective ways to develop technology strategies because such an approach is not cost-effective.

Daniel, a staunch proponent of the electronic revolution in education, holds the position that it takes a village to educate a student, but the villagers are not primarily teachers because teachers represent an enormous cost in "delivering" education. Rather, the villagers are a host of support people who will orchestrate learning in ways that are quite different from the traditional notions of education. Hanly (1998) notes that an online course "takes a team of academics and techies—not to mention the financial commitment from the school—to make it happen" (p. 1). Yet, as I will show in my third criticism, the motivating force behind the electronic revolution in higher education is not pedagogy but economics, the very reason Daniel gives for eschewing the laissez-faire approach. As Feenberg (1999) says, "Pedagogical objectives take the back seat to prestige and budgetary ones" (p. 5).

Criticism Three

Therefore, I contend that the academy has adopted the entrepreneurial impulse for economic gain, an impulse that overrides the integrity of the academic mission to support the acquisition of knowledge through rigorous research. The impulse for economic gain that drives the burgeoning call for online courses is primarily concerned with profit, not learning, with economic gain, not vigorous, professional research that informs sound pedagogy.

Anyone who reads much about computer technology and higher education finds that the literature constantly refers to economics and competition. For example, Michael Leavitt, a leading proponent of the Western Virtual University, freely admits that the electronic revolution in higher education is being propelled by the marketplace. Leavitt says, "There's more driving this than higher education. It's the marketplace" (Finney, 1996, p. 3). David Noble, an ardent opponent of advocates like Leavitt, nevertheless agrees that the marketplace, including corporations that want to make money from selling education packaged in technological garb, is driving the electronic revolution in higher education. Noble (1998b) refers to the economic impulse behind the electronic revolution in education as "commercial motives and preoccupations" (p. 1).

Noble is considerably less sanguine than Leavitt about the results of such market forces. He believes that the outcome is "the commercialization of higher education" (1998a, p. 3), which will result in what Taylor (1998) calls training, not education: "The threat of the new technologies is that profit-seeking firms will use them to bring us something that is called higher education but is in reality training" (p. 3). Why? Because as Taylor points out, speaking for academicians, for-profit private sector firms "do not share our ethics, our values, or our concept of what constitutes higher education" (p. 5). Thompson (1998) articulates those values when he says that the tools touted in the "digital reform of education . . . must subordinate themselves to the ends for which the university was created. Those ends are: to civilize the young, to fit them for the professions, and to prepare them for governing themselves" (p. 7). Worthy ends indeed, but not the ends for which those who seek to commercialize the university strive. Their goal is profit, with little if any genuine regard for educational quality. Educational convenience, yes. Educational cost savings, yes. Educational quality? No.

Why not? Educational quality requires a learned professorate, and the digital reform of education, if it hopes to achieve the utopia some predict, must wrest control of the curriculum from the professorate so that educational products can be delivered cheaply (translate: profitably) by inexpensive labor. As Feenberg (1999) says, "A straight route down the information superhighway leads from the deprofessionalization to the deskilling of higher education" (p. 4). In speaking of the incursion of electronic technology into the academy, Mitchell (1999) notes that universities "urgently need to recover full power to control their educational philosophy and ethos and to determine what and how they teach by reference to stable, objective academic principles" (p. 22).

Perhaps the greatest irony of the digital reform of education is that the academy sold itself to for-profit organizations that promised economic riches at the expense of academic integrity. I have said that the academy sold out to for-profit organizations, but I need to be more precise. The administrators of the academy sold out, a point Noble (1998a) makes when he says, "It is no accident, then, that the high-tech transformation of higher education is being initiated and implemented from the top down, either without any student and faculty involvement in the decision making or despite it" (p. 2). One irony of the top-down approach, the nonconsultative management style, is that the practitioners of the approach are trained as academics and most have professorial experience and rank. Those who occupy the primary positions in academic service—presidents, chancellors, provosts—have betrayed the spirit and principles of their vocation. As Thompson (1998) notes, "The new dedication to computer-assisted learning strikes me as something akin to a crass religious cult. . . . Idolatrous faith that computers will save Western civilization threatens to become the conventional wisdom" (p. 3). The false apostles of this idolatrous faith are the brethren who have exchanged academic regalia for priestly garments composed of three-piece suits. And they don't need pesky faculty interfering with contractual arrangements with for-profit organizations that promise an economic mecca. However, they do need faculty to provide the intellectual content that can be fed into the technological machine, a machine that is like an idol.

Ways to Redress the Breach of Ethics

I offer this section knowing that the academy is already waist-deep in the technology revolution and wading deeper daily. My suggestions for redressing the problems that I have discussed will require drastic action, if they are to be heeded at all. I will address first administrators and then professors. To administrators I recommend the following:

- Stop using economic arguments as the primary or sole criteria for making programmatic decisions about technology. Programmatic decisions should always include concerns about quality of education; economic arguments are only part of any decision about quality.
- Fund studies of online courses that are grounded in established educational theory and use rigorous, widely accepted methodologies.
- Return to faculty the right and responsibility to determine pedagogical issues related to the use of technology in classrooms. The faculty should have the authority to determine curricular issues that involve the use of technology in classrooms, whether those classrooms are on the campus or in nontraditional, metaphorical "classrooms" created by online courses.
- Provide adequate faculty development opportunities for faculty who seek to teach online courses *before* they teach those courses.
- Count the costs of online courses (including start-up costs, upgrades, maintenance, technical support, and replacement costs) and make sure those costs can be covered so that faculty are not hostage to technology that cannot be used adequately because the technology budget is insufficient.

To faculty I recommend the following:

- Conduct studies of online courses that are grounded in established educational theory and use rigorous, widely accepted methodologies. Seek institutional funding for those studies. If the administration is not willing to fund those studies and yet endorses online courses, then assume that the administration is not interested in maintaining the integrity of academic ethics concerning the academic contract with students and professors.
- Resist any coercive efforts to compromise academic standards at the expense of faulty arguments about the supposed economic gains attributed to online courses.
- Be wary of attempts by the academy or any external organization to lay claim to your intellectual property rights. If faculty do not resist such attempts, they will be contributing to the ethical breach.

Conclusion

For some, this article will appear out of place in a volume dedicated to information about how professors can be effective in the online classroom. What I have said may appear to negate the advice of the other authors, who promote online classrooms. As an academic, I am dedicated to the expression of a full range of ideas about a topic, and what I have said should not be interpreted to mean that I am in principle opposed to the use of technology in higher education, or even to the existence of online classrooms. Rather, I am concerned that the establishment of online courses be in accord with good academic practice. My concern is that no student or professor be held hostage to false claims about the digital reform of higher education. I am concerned that the integrity of the academic enterprise not be compromised under the guise of educational progress that is driven primarily—perhaps solely—by economic gain.

References

Audi, R. (1994). On the ethics of teaching and the ideals of learning. *Academe, 80*(5), 27–36.

Cahn, S. M. (Ed.). (1990). *Morality, responsibility, and the university: Studies in academic ethics.* Philadelphia: Temple University Press.

Daniel, J. S. (1997). Why universities need technology strategies. *Change, 29*(4), 11–17.

Erhmann, S. C. (1999). Asking hard questions about technology use and education. *Change, 31*(2), 25–29.

Feenberg, A. (1999). *Distance learning: Promise or threat?* [http://www.rohan.sdsu.edu/faculty/feenberg/TELE3.htm].

Finney, J. E. (1996). An interview: Michael A. Leavitt. *Crosstalk, 4*(2), 2–3.

Fisch, L. (Ed.). (1996). *Ethical dimensions of college and university teaching: Understanding and honoring the special relationship between teachers and students.* New Directions for Teaching and Learning, no. 66. San Francisco: Jossey-Bass.

Green, K. C. (1999). When wishes come true: Colleges and the convergence of access, lifelong learning, and technology. *Change, 31*(2), 11–15.

Hanly, B. (1998). Online ed 101. *Wired News.* [www.wired.com/news/news/email/explode-infobeat/culture/story/15061.html].

Kidder, R. M. (1995). The ethics of teaching and the teaching of ethics. In E. Boschmann (Ed.), *The electronic classroom: A handbook for education in the electronic environment* (pp. 222–227). Medford, NJ: Learned Information.

Merisotis, J. P., & Phipps, R. A. (1999). What's the difference? Outcomes of distance vs. traditional classroom-based learning. *Change, 31*(3), 13–17.

Mitchell, T. N. (1999). From Plato to the Internet. *Change, 31*(2), 17–22.

Noble, D. F. (1998a). Digital diploma mills: The automation of higher education. *First Monday.* [http://www.firstmonday.dk/issues/issue3_1/noble/].

Noble, D. F. (1998b). Digital diploma mills. Part II: The coming battle over online instruction. [http://www.uwo.ca/uwofa/articles/di_dip_2.html].

Ryan, J.J.C.H. (1999). Student plagiarism in an online world. *Prism.* [http://www.asee.org/prism/december/html/student_plagiarism_in_an_onlin.html].

Taylor, K. S. (1998). Higher education: From craft-production to capitalist enterprise? *First Monday.* [http://www.firstmonday.dk/issues/issue3_9/taylor/index.html].

Thompson, T. H. (1998). Three futures of the electronic university: To dream the possible dream. *Educom Review, 33*(2), 1–9. [http://www.educause./edu/pub/er.review/.reviewArticles.33234.html].

BRUCE W. SPECK *is Dean for the College of Arts and Sciences at the University of North Carolina at Pembroke.*

11 *Optimism about the potential digital reform of higher education must be tempered by concerns about student learning.*

Epilogue: A Cautionary Note About Online Classrooms

R. W. Carstens, Victor L. Worsfold

Can liberal learning be sustained through technology, specifically in the online classroom? Our conclusion is that it is very difficult to do so because the technology that connects individuals in the online classroom vitiates the personal and intellectual experiences that are so essential to an education. Simply put, the technology of the online classroom does not allow for the personal transformation that is a necessary part of learning. We support this conclusion by first offering a definition of liberal learning, which, in our view, is the goal of education. Second, we describe the nature of the online classroom and examine the degree to which it can sustain liberal learning. Finally, we discuss essential elements for learning that are eliminated in the online classroom.

What Is Liberal Learning?

Although our conclusion described in the previous paragraph may seem to reflect the judgment of Luddites, it is a judgment rooted in an understanding of the very purpose of liberal learning: "To learn to be human is to develop through the give-and-take of communication" (Dewey, 1954, p. 154).

Liberal learning is essential to the health of society because liberal education is one of the primary means through which individuals develop their own personhood, and such development has as its foundational value and goal the freedom whereby students make choices that contribute to their personal well-being. Freedom and personhood are dimensions of the same ontological reality. The community in which people develop as free and informed beings affects the nature and content of their lives. If a person does not have the chance to choose and the chance to learn with others, that person is diminished. Thus, a society—educational or otherwise—that is worthy of people holds liberal education paramount.

Nussbaum (1997) adds another dimension to the notion of becoming educated: "Becoming . . . educated . . . means learning lots of facts and mastering techniques of reasoning. But it means something more. It means learning how to be a human being capable of love and imagination" (p. 14).

Can the Online Classroom Sustain Liberal Learning?

Technology is not merely instrumental but laden with values that mitigate against liberal learning. To understand this idea, it is necessary to understand the nature and purpose of the online classroom.

Philosophers have long been aware that the way we use tools informs how we define and become ourselves (for example, Ellul, 1964; Oppenheimer, 1997). Tools, moreover, change human beings in terms of their social evolution. By its very structure, the human brain possesses the ability to develop new combinations of old and new types of neural networks, and this capacity is in large part the result of the environment in which the brain develops (Healy, 1990). Thus, we conclude that technology—as a tool—is inherently value-laden. We also argue that its primary values are in administrative efficiency and institutional economic ambition—two concepts that may be in stark contrast to learning.

It is the conflict between the definition of liberal learning and the values inherent in the online classroom that creates the tension. If we believe that the goal of liberal education is the achievement of human excellence resulting from personal gifts translated through education into actions appropriate to individuals but always reconciled through community, then it seems that the values of efficiency and true liberal learning may be at odds (Bromley, 1998).

What Is the Intellectual Cost of the Online Classroom?

The cost of the online classroom can be most obviously seen in the elimination of the interpersonal role of teachers and students and the elimination of an environment where students are required to engage in legitimate exercises of literacy.

Elimination of the Interpersonal. Clearly, the online classroom eliminates the value of personal relationships in the name of efficiency. As a result, educational and other cultural values are degraded. For example, the personal freedom that comes from learning through the intellectual demands of social exchange and peer collaboration with other students no longer exists. The critical ability to question the authority of those who teach and the capacity to argue a position until its weaknesses are exposed are no longer part of classroom dialogues.

Examining the online classroom in more antiseptic terms yields similar conclusions. Digital knowledge is "knowledge that is explicit and can be reduced to discrete bits of data which can be stored on a massive scale [and] manipulated in complex ways" (Bowers, 1988, p. 33). The implication of Bowers's statement is that the computer transmits knowledge to students using formal rules in the form of algorithms. These rules do not allow students to question the interpretation (or offer alternative interpretations) of knowledge presented by the computer's programmer. The computer, moreover, by its very mode of transmission denies the validity of other modes of interpersonal knowledge transmission, such as body language and dialogue. The computer conceives intelligence as "individualistic in nature, its highest expression . . . viewed as involving procedural thinking whereby data and simulations are to be dealt with at an abstract, decontextualized level" (Bromley, 1988, p. 90). The computer's vaunted encouragement of individualism leads to isolation.

Elimination of Student Literacy. If technology is never merely instrumental, then the impact of various technologies must be considered. Overreliance on visual culture (videos, TV, video games, computers) short-circuits the brain development necessary for literacy, as well as critical and abstract thinking (Healy, 1990). And even more sobering is the problem of the banished imagination. Students today, and many professors, have little or no imagination because their culture presents their own experiences through someone else's visualization. Today's learners are afflicted by the lack of real experiences in childhood as they depend more and more on visualization and less on literacy and language (Healy, 1990).

Even the types of literacy that technology fosters are inferior. For example, e-mail is a marvelous means of communication, but it is not the same thing as face-to-face interaction, especially in the matter of thinking. E-mail is not even the same as writing in the liberal arts sense because most of the messages sent are neither composed nor structured. The "rough draft" nature of most e-mail messages limits writing as a valuable tool for communication. Computers can teach facts efficiently and provide drills for some techniques of reasoning, but they cannot teach what Nussbaum (1997) and others understand as Socratic self-examination and narrative imagination.

Recall the most famous passage of Socrates' *Apology*: "The unexamined life is not worth living for a human being" (Nussbaum, 1997, p. 15). To be sure, a computer can tell a student that this is what Socrates said, can even explain what commentators believe Socrates was trying to achieve in uttering it, but the "most important ingredient of a Socratic classroom is the instructor" (p. 41). No computer yet possesses the expertise required of Socratic professors to teach each student about leading the examined life and belonging to a community that encourages self-examination each day. The personal interconnection of professor with student and student with student is vital for Socratic teaching to be successful—personal interconnection that encourages self-examination and its concomitant self-criticism in the security of a community of trusting, self-seeking individuals. And if such an environment is necessary for self-examination, it may be doubly so as students begin to tackle the questions that arise in their quest for world citizenship—a quest that will be so vital for students in the twenty-first century.

Narrative imagination (Nussbaum, 1997) is the foundational skill of moral imagination. When students read about or write from a perspective not their own, they have experiences of receptivity and voice that are essential to their own self-examination. Such experiences in critical self-examination—which exercises in narrative imagination provide—quickly become a moral exercise because students come to see characters alien to their culture as their equals and are confronted with the need to treat them fairly, respecting them and reading their lives as they themselves read them. Critical self-examination and the examination of others in the course of becoming world citizens, which narrative imagination helps realize, underscore the moral dimension of liberal learning. Even the most sophisticated computer program cannot explicitly inculcate in a morally appropriate way the moral stance required by the pursuit of a liberal education—namely, the ability to treat others as equals.

Language really is the architect of culture, and language becomes higher thinking only when it goes beyond pictures. We begin to think conceptually and abstractly when we go beyond the chatter of naming things and manipulating information and come to a syntax that not only defines but also relates things as concepts and concepts as abstract vocabulary. Student inability to think critically seems to be directly related to the visualization of their culture. They are rarely required to think abstractly because most visual media simplify the depth of communication by picturing things. Interconnection skills developed from critically listening to stories is never required. Students have difficulty solving problems, reasoning sequentially and abstractly, and thus writing coherently because they are literally and figuratively overstimulated by visual culture. We also know that there is a relationship between TV viewing and passive brains (see Healy, 1990). This, in turn, leads to a decline in the ability to remain focused and a decline in the development of skills that derive from being focused on the task at hand (listening, reading for understanding, abstracting meaning, and using language effectively). The similarities between TVs and computers seem obvious. At risk are "higher-ordered organizational abilities, including the all-important control, motivation, and planning functions" (Healy, 1990, p. 216).

The online classroom relies on individualized learning through visualization and the use of written, often uncomposed, language. Will the online classroom be able to remedy the illiteracy and aliteracy of contemporary students? Or will their e-mail messages, which are written but not writing in the liberal arts sense, become the standard of the written word? Internet travel can be enriching only if the travelers know languages, know them well, and also know how to judge the authoritativeness of those whom they meet along the way. Our caution is that these issues, which can be assessed and remedied through the interpersonal exchanges so essential to the liberal arts classroom, may mean that online classrooms perpetuate the deficiencies in contemporary students. Indeed, the model of education that will be derived from the online classroom and its technology may be mere knowledge transfer rather than personal transformation and the development of human values.

Conclusion

Ultimately, the religion of technology stands as evidence of the triumph of nineteenth-century materialism—the philosophical stance that holds that only the material, empirical order is real and valuable. If people and the communities in which they dwell are merely malleable bits of matter, then freedom and the questions that obtain are moot. What educational technology has shown to those of us who engage in the kind of teaching that suggests there is more to the human than meets the eye, that there are values that transcend material circumstance, is that some can see what most do not: that education driven by technology, although perhaps beneficial in some regards, is insufficient for truly human beings to develop, and perhaps even dangerous to our future.

References

Bowers, C. A. (1988). *The cultural dimensions of educational computing: Understanding the nonneutrality of technology.* New York: Teachers College Press.

Bromley, H. (1998). How to tell if you really need the latest technology. *Thought and Action, 14*(1) 21–28.

Dewey, J. (1954). *The public and its problems.* Chicago: Swallow Press.

Ellul, J. (1964). *The technological society.* (J. Wilkinson, Trans.). New York: Vintage Books.

Healy, J. M. (1990). *Endangered minds: Why our children don't think.* New York: Simon & Schuster.

Nussbaum, M. C. (1997). *Cultivating humanity: A classical defense of reform in liberal education.* Cambridge, MA: Harvard University Press.

Oppenheimer, T. (1997, July). The computer delusion. *Atlantic Monthly,* pp. 45–63.

R. W. CARSTENS teaches humanities and political science at Ohio Dominican College in Columbus and is also director of its humanities program.

VICTOR L. WORSFOLD teaches philosophy, humanities, and education at the University of Texas at Dallas and is director of its Teaching Quality Enhancement Program.

INDEX

Back Issue/Subscription Order Form

Copy or detach and send to:
Jossey-Bass Inc., 350 Sansome Street, San Francisco CA 94104-1342

Call or fax toll free!
Phone 888-378-2537 6AM-5PM PST; Fax 800-605-2665

Back issues: Please send me the following issues at $23 each
(Important: please include series initials and issue number, such as TL90)

1. TL _____

_____

_____

$ _____ Total for single issues

$ _____ Shipping charges (for single issues *only;* subscriptions are exempt
from shipping charges): Up to $30, add $5^{50} • $30^{01}–$50, add $6^{50}
$50^{01}–$75, add $8 • $75^{01}–$100, add $10 • $100^{01}–$150, add $12
Over $150, call for shipping charge

Subscriptions   Please ❏ start   ❏ renew my subscription to *New Directions for
Teaching and Learning* for the year _____ at the following rate:

U.S.:	❏ Individual $58	❏ Institutional $104
Canada:	❏ Individual $83	❏ Institutional $129
All Others:	❏ Individual $88	❏ Institutional $134

NOTE: Subscriptions are quarterly, and are for the calendar year only.
Subscriptions begin with the Spring issue of the year indicated above.

$ _____ Total single issues and subscriptions (Add appropriate sales tax
for your state for single issue orders. No sales tax for U.S. subscriptions.
Canadian residents, add GST for subscriptions and single issues.)

❏ Payment enclosed (U.S. check or money order only)

❏ VISA, MC, AmEx, Discover Card #_____ Exp. date_____

Signature _____ Day phone _____

❏ Bill me (U.S. institutional orders only. Purchase order required)

Purchase order #_____

Federal Tax ID 135593032   GST 89102-8052

Name _____

Address _____

_____

Phone_____ E-mail _____

For more information about Jossey-Bass, visit our Web site at:
www.josseybass.com   **PRIORITY CODE = ND1**

OTHER TITLES AVAILABLE IN THE
NEW DIRECTIONS FOR TEACHING AND LEARNING SERIES
Marilla D. Svinicki, Editor-in-Chief
R. Eugene Rice, Consulting Editor

United States Postal Service
Statement of Ownership, Management, and Circulation

| 1. Publication Title | New Directions For Teaching And Learning | 2. Publication Number 0 2 7 1 – 0 6 3 3 | 3. Filing Date 9/29/00 |

| 4. Issue Frequency | Quarterly | 5. Number of Issues Published Annually 4 | 6. Annual Subscription Price $59 – Individual $114 – Institution |

7. Complete Mailing Address of Known Office of Publication (Not printer) (Street, city, county, state, and ZIP+4)
350 Sansome Street
San Francisco, CA 94104
(San Francisco County)

Contact Person: Joe Schuman
Telephone: 415-782-3232

8. Complete Mailing Address of Headquarters or General Business Office of Publisher (Not printer)

Same As Above

9. Full Names and Complete Mailing Addresses of Publisher, Editor, and Managing Editor (Do not leave blank)
Publisher (Name and complete mailing address)

Jossey-Bass, A Wiley Company
Above Address

Editor (Name and complete mailing address)

Marilla D. Svinicki
Center for Teaching Effectiveness/Univ. of Texas@Austin
Main Building 2200
Austin, TX 78712-1111

Managing Editor (Name and complete mailing address)

None

10. Owner (Do not leave blank. If the publication is owned by a corporation, give the name and address of the corporation immediately followed by the names and addresses of all stockholders owning or holding 1 percent or more of the total amount of stock. If not owned by a corporation, give the names and addresses of the individual owners. If owned by a partnership or other unincorporated firm, give its name and address as well as those of each individual owner. If the publication is published by a nonprofit organization, give its name and address.)

Full Name	Complete Mailing Address
John Wiley & Sons Inc.	605 Third Avenue New York, NY 10158-0012

11. Known Bondholders, Mortgagees, and Other Security Holders Owning or Holding 1 Percent or More of Total Amount of Bonds, Mortgages, or Other Securities. If none, check box → ☐ None

Full Name	Complete Mailing Address
Same As Above	Same As Above

12. Tax Status (For completion by nonprofit organizations authorized to mail at nonprofit rates) (Check one)
The purpose, function, and nonprofit status of this organization and the exempt status for federal income tax purposes:
☐ Has Not Changed During Preceding 12 Months
☐ Has Changed During Preceding 12 Months (Publisher must submit explanation of change with this statement)

PS Form 3526, October 1999   (See Instructions on Reverse)

---

13. Publication Title	New Directions For Teaching And Learning	14. Issue Date for Circulation Data Below Summer 2000	
15.	Extent and Nature of Circulation	Average No. Copies Each Issue During Preceding 12 Months	No. Copies of Single Issue Published Nearest to Filing Date
a. Total Number of Copies (Net press run)		1,902	2,156
b. Paid and/or Requested Circulation (1)	Paid/Requested Outside-County Mail Subscriptions Stated on Form 3541. (Include advertiser's proof and exchange copies)	847	768
(2)	Paid In-County Subscriptions Stated on Form 3541 (Include advertiser's proof and exchange copies)	0	0
(3)	Sales Through Dealers and Carriers, Street Vendors, Counter Sales, and Other Non-USPS Paid Distribution	0	0
(4)	Other Classes Mailed Through the USPS	0	0
c. Total Paid and/or Requested Circulation [Sum of 15b. (1), (2), (3), and (4)] ▶		847	768
d. Free Distribution by Mail (Samples, complimentary, and other free) (1)	Outside-County as Stated on Form 3541	1	1
(2)	In-County as Stated on Form 3541	0	0
(3)	Other Classes Mailed Through the USPS	0	0
e. Free Distribution Outside the Mail (Carriers or other means)		57	47
f. Total Free Distribution (Sum of 15d. and 15e.) ▶		58	48
g. Total Distribution (Sum of 15c. and 15f.) ▶		905	816
h. Copies not Distributed		997	1,340
i. Total (Sum of 15g. and h.) ▶		1,902	2,156
j. Percent Paid and/or Requested Circulation (15c. divided by 15g. times 100)		94%	94%

16. Publication of Statement of Ownership
☒ Publication required. Will be printed in the __Winter 2000__ issue of this publication.   ☐ Publication not required.

17. Signature and Title of Editor, Publisher, Business Manager, or Owner _Susan E. Lewis_ Vice President & Publisher Periodicals   Date 9/29/00

I certify that all information furnished on this form is true and complete. I understand that anyone who furnishes false or misleading information on this form or who omits material or information requested on the form may be subject to criminal sanctions (including fines and imprisonment) and/or civil sanctions (including civil penalties).

Instructions to Publishers

1. Complete and file one copy of this form with your postmaster annually on or before October 1. Keep a copy of the completed form for your records.

2. In cases where the stockholder or security holder is a trustee, include in items 10 and 11 the name of the person or corporation for whom the trustee is acting. Also include the names and addresses of individuals who are stockholders who own or hold 1 percent or more of the total amount of bonds, mortgages, or other securities of the publishing corporation. In item 11, if none, check the box. Use blank sheets if more space is required.

3. Be sure to furnish all circulation information called for in item 15. Free circulation must be shown in items 15d, e, and f.

4. Item 15h., Copies not Distributed, must include (1) newsstand copies originally stated on Form 3541, and returned to the publisher, (2) estimated returns from news agents, and (3), copies for office use, leftovers, spoiled, and all other copies not distributed.

5. If the publication had Periodicals authorization as a general or requester publication, this Statement of Ownership, Management, and Circulation must be published; it must be printed in any issue in October or, if the publication is not published during October, the first issue printed after October.

6. In item 16, indicate the date of the issue in which this Statement of Ownership will be published.

7. Item 17 must be signed.

Failure to file or publish a statement of ownership may lead to suspension of Periodicals authorization.

PS Form 3526, October 1999 (Reverse)